NEW DIRECTIONS FOR CHILD AND ADOLESCENT DEVELOPMENT

William Damon, *Stanford University*
EDITOR-IN-CHIEF

Family Obligation and Assistance During Adolescence

Contextual Variations and Developmental Implications

Andrew J. Fuligni
New York University

EDITOR

Number 94, Winter 2001

JOSSEY-BASS
A Wiley Company
www.josseybass.com

FAMILY OBLIGATION AND ASSISTANCE DURING ADOLESCENCE: CONTEXTUAL
VARIATIONS AND DEVELOPMENTAL IMPLICATIONS
Andrew J. Fuligni (ed.)
New Directions for Child and Adolescent Development, no. 94
William Damon, Editor-in-Chief

Microfilm copies of issues and articles are available in 16mm and 35mm,
as well as microfiche in 105mm, through University Microfilms Inc., 300
North Zeeb Road, Ann Arbor, MI 48106.

ISSN 1520-3247   electronic ISSN 1534-8687   ISBN 0-7879-5778-X

NEW DIRECTIONS FOR CHILD AND ADOLESCENT DEVELOPMENT is part of
The Jossey-Bass Education Series and is published quarterly by Jossey-Bass,
989 Market Street, San Francisco, CA 94103-1741. Periodicals postage paid
at San Francisco, California, and at additional mailing offices. Postmaster:
Send address changes to New Directions for Child and Adolescent Development, Jossey-Bass, 989 Market Street, San Francisco, CA 94103-1741.

New Directions for Child and Adolescent Development is indexed in Bio-
sciences Information Service, Current Index to Journals in Education
(ERIC), Psychological Abstracts, and Sociological Abstracts.

SUBSCRIPTIONS cost $75.00 for individuals and $125.00 for institutions,
agencies, and libraries.

EDITORIAL CORRESPONDENCE should be sent to the Editor-in-Chief,
William Damon, Stanford Center on Adolescence, Cypress Building C,
Stanford University, Stanford, CA 94305.

Cover photograph by Wernher Krutein/PHOTOVAULT © 1990.

Jossey-Bass Web address: www.josseybass.com

Printed in the United States of America on acid-free recycled paper containing 100 percent recovered waste paper, of which at least 20 percent is
postconsumer waste.

Contents

EDITOR'S NOTES   1
Andrew J. Fuligni

1. Work Contributions to the Family: Developing a   5
Conceptual and Research Framework
Jacqueline J. Goodnow, Jeanette A. Lawrence
The study of work contributions to the family should pay attention to
differences in the type of contributions made, the impact of various cir-
cumstances, and the feelings people express about such contributions.

2. Household Chores: Under What Conditions   23
Do Mothers Lean on Daughters?
Ann C. Crouter, Melissa R. Head, Matthew F. Bumpus, Susan M. McHale
Daughters bear the brunt of extra housework when mothers work in
demanding jobs, even when they have older brothers who might be
expected to share in the work because of their greater level of maturity.

3. Extended Schooling, Adolescence, and the   43
Renegotiation of Responsibility Among Italian Immigrant
Families in New Haven, Connecticut, 1910–1940
Stephen Lassonde
The American introduction of universal secondary schooling in the early
twentieth century collided with traditional notions of family responsi-
bility among southern Italian immigrants, who expected their adoles-
cents to work in order to contribute to the subsistence of the family.

4. Family Obligation and the Academic Motivation   61
of Adolescents from Asian, Latin American, and
European Backgrounds
Andrew J. Fuligni
Adolescents from Asian and Latin American families in the United
States have a strong sense of obligation to the family, and their sense of
familial duty is associated with a specific belief in the importance and
usefulness of education.

5. Children Investing in Their Families: The Importance of   77
Child Obligation in Successful Development
Thomas S. Weisner
The findings of the previous chapters are discussed in terms of the role
that youths' obligations play in the overall adaptive strategies of families.

INDEX   85

EDITOR'S NOTES

In comparison to the emotional attachment of adolescents to their parents, more instrumental forms of youths' connection to the family have received less attention in mainstream developmental research on adolescents. Rather than being considered fundamental developmental phenomena, adolescents' contributions and obligations to the family have been studied as issues relevant only for specific segments of the population and during selected periods in history. This may be due to a number of factors, ranging from the legacy of the psychoanalytic focus on dyadic attachment and conflict between parents and children to the current conception of children in postindustrial societies as being "precious" rather than "useful" to the family. Whatever the reason, current scholarly discourse rarely includes duty and obligation as fundamental concerns in family relationships during adolescence.

This volume, based on a symposium presented at the 2000 Biennial Meeting of the Society for Research on Adolescence, draws together work done among diverse populations with different methods in order to begin treating family assistance and obligation as a focused area of study. The chapter authors transcend their specific areas of inquiry and consider the broader developmental implications of their findings. Collectively, the chapters address two basic questions: What contextual factors, broadly conceived, give rise to variations in family assistance and obligation during adolescence? and What are the implications of family assistance and obligation for other aspects of adolescents' development? Each chapter by itself provides specific answers to these questions in terms of its area of focus, and together they offer some basic working principles to guide the study of family assistance and obligation more generally.

Jacqueline Goodnow and Jeanette Lawrence begin by offering a broad conceptual framework that could be applied to the study of any type of work contribution to the family. Noting a disunity in the perspectives on children's work contributions across different areas of research, they suggest that the study of family assistance and obligation would profit by following three principles: (1) moving toward an enriched description of contributions made or expected, (2) considering the impact of various circumstances, and (3) taking a closer look at the feelings people express about their work contributions. Although Goodnow and Lawrence discuss how these three principles have aided their specific work on the social distribution of household chores, the applicability of these principles is much broader. By following these three principles, developmentalists will gain a better appreciation of how concerns about adolescents' assistance and obligation are embedded in the relationships within most families and carry with them some of the most fundamental socialization goals of parents.

Ann Crouter, Melissa Head, Matthew Bumpus, and Susan McHale follow in Chapter Two with a systematic investigation of how maternal employment shapes the gender distribution of household chores. Going beyond the traditional yet uninformative dichotomy between mothers who work and do not work outside the home, Crouter and her colleagues examine variations in the demands of mothers' jobs. Their results point to the power of both parental occupations and gender in the distribution of household chores. Girls, but not boys, take up the slack when their mothers work in high-stress jobs. Even girls with older brothers do more household work in these conditions. This fascinating in-depth analysis highlights how a factor such as maternal employment, which might be expected to affect family assistance in one direction, actually has the opposite effect on the social distribution of chores because of another powerful factor: gender roles. The findings of this investigation highlight the importance of considering how multiple contextual factors work in concert with one another rather than in isolation.

In Chapter Three, Stephen Lassonde employs the tools of a social historian to examine what happens when changing social institutions challenge how cultures traditionally define the duties and responsibilities of adolescents to the family. Immigrant families from southern Italy settling in New Haven, Connecticut, early in the twentieth century found themselves in one of the more dramatic social changes in American history. The spread of universal secondary schooling reflected a rapid extension of childhood within the United States, a trend that clashed with the immigrants' belief that teenagers were actually adults who needed to contribute to the subsistence of the family. What is perhaps most remarkable about Lassonde's analysis is that despite the extent to which the immigrants' views were tied to beliefs about morality, gender, and marriage, the inexorable force of the American educational system served to weaken their traditions so that only twenty to thirty years after immigration, virtually all of the teenagers in this ethnic group were attending secondary school. Such is the power of widespread social institutions to shape the construction of adolescents' duties and obligations to the family.

In a companion to Lassonde's piece, I analyze the extent to which a sense of family obligation is connected to academic motivation among immigrant and ethnic minority groups in the contemporary United States. In contrast to Lassonde, I find that a sense of family obligation is related to stronger academic motivation among youths. In fact, the greater familial duty among teenagers from Asian and Latin American societies leads them to possess a stronger belief in the importance and utility of education than their equally achieving peers from European backgrounds. Together, Chapters Three and Four provide strong evidence for the power of the educational system in a society in the construction of the responsibilities of youths. In contemporary American society, the link between education and occupational success is well proven, and immigrants today are fully aware of the critical importance of their adolescents' educational attainment for the economic well-being of both the adolescent and the family. One suspects that had Lassonde's Italian immigrants arrived in the United States during the current period of few economic opportunities for those without a high school diploma, they too would have linked youths' family obligations with staying in school.

Finally, Thomas Weisner discusses how the obligations of children and adolescents to contribute to the family are fundamental elements in the overall adaptive strategy of families and how familial duties link general developmental processes with the context of a particular historical moment and a specific cultural community.

I am grateful for the support of a William T. Grant Foundation Faculty Scholars Award and a FIRST Award from the National Institute of Child Health and Human Development during the preparation of this volume. I also thank Jacqueline Goodnow and Ann Crouter for encouraging me to put together this volume in the *New Directions for Child and Adolescent Development* series.

Andrew J. Fuligni
Editor

ANDREW J. FULIGNI is associate professor of psychology at New York University.

1

This chapter proposes ways to enrich our descriptions of work, bring out the impact of various circumstances, and link work contributions to ideas and feelings about family membership and family relationships.

Work Contributions to the Family: Developing a Conceptual and Research Framework

Jacqueline J. Goodnow, Jeanette A. Lawrence

This chapter proposes a particular way of looking at contributions to the functioning or the economy of a family. This framework is applicable to any family member and to contributions of any kind. The application here, however, is to contributions that are made by children and, especially, adolescents and are of the kind known as chores, jobs, or household work.

The search for a general framework is sparked by two concerns. One is the need for a closer fit between the data and the concepts usually brought to bear on work contributions by children and adolescents. The other is a concern with the tendency to treat these contributions in isolation. In principle, the ways in which we think about work contributions by children and adolescents should be extendable to the contributions made by adults in couple relationships or in the course of caregiving for a parent in need of assistance. In practice, those interconnections are seldom made. In principle also, the ways in which we think about work contributions should be extendable to other contributions: contributions, for example, of love, money, respect, obedience, or upholding the honor of the family. In practice, those interconnections are seldom made.

This chapter owes a great deal to discussions with Jennifer Bowes, Judy Cashmore, Joan Grusec, Andrew Fuligni, and Pamela Warton. The preparation of the chapter was aided financially by a grant from the Australian Research Council to us, assistance that we happily acknowledge.

Our use of the term *contributions* is a deliberate step toward reducing this conceptual isolation and toward opening up new questions. We avoid the term *chores,* for example, partly because the term is less widely used in Australia than the term *job* or *work* and partly because *chore* has the overtone of something onerous and imposed. That quality need not be present. In contrast, the term *contributions* allows for offerings that may come about in several ways: spontaneously, after various kinds of negotiation, or under various forms of pressure. It also prompts questions about possible substitutions. If I prefer not to make this kind of contribution, is some other contribution acceptable? Can I, for example, substitute one kind of work for another? Can I do less household work if I make a stronger commitment to doing well at school or start contributing money to the family? Finally, the term *contributions* fits a view of families as involving some particular obligations. They are groups in which, to use a phrase we often heard from parents, "everyone puts in something."

We outline the background to the search for a framework and then describe some research steps and conceptual proposals that serve as the core of an overall framework. These proposals have to do with the nature of contributions, the impact of various circumstances, and the significance of the family setting. In illustrating these steps and proposals in practice, we draw especially on a series of studies that focused on a particular quality of work contributions: the extent to which they are movable from one family member to another. We end with some further research possibilities and ask what might now be suggested with regard to the impact of a particular pair of circumstances: the potential contributor is in the age period known as adolescence or youth, and the setting is one of family.

Work Contributions: A Variety of Perspectives

Researchers, and family members too, may frame work contributions in a variety of ways, from labors of love or necessity to questions of duty or forms of oppression.

Among researchers, for example, work contributions by children and adolescents have been seen as a form of child labor (Straus, 1962), a "nascent prosocial activity" (Rheingold, 1982), a basis for learning about responsibility (Staub, 1979), an indication of historical changes in the position and value of children (Zelizer, 1985), an introduction to gendered divisions of work (Berk, 1985), and an area in which one can observe how competence emerges in the course of "guided participation" (Rogoff, Mistry, Goncu, and Mosier, 1993). Each researcher appears to work within one way of framing the topic, ignoring the others (Goodnow, 1988).

Each possibility, moreover, turns out to have some difficulties in its fit with the data. Accounts in terms of the development of responsibility or prosocial behavior, for example, fit well with the kinds of phrases that Anglo Australian mothers used in our studies when we asked them about the age at which they expect children to take on some "regular household jobs" (the target children were five to six years of age) (Goodnow, Cashmore, Cotton, and Knight, 1984). Some job, even if small in scope, was seen as "good for children" and as "developing a sense of responsibility." Accounts in terms of responsibility also have a moderate fit with data showing that among Australian and Canadian children, work contributions of a particular type—done regularly and self-regulated rather than being done on request or after reminders—are, at least by ages ten to twelve, correlated with helpfulness within the family although not outside it (Grusec, Goodnow, and Cohen, 1996).

An emphasis on responsibility, however, does not fit well with the answers given by Lebanese Australian mothers (Lebanese born and now living in Australia) to questions about an age for household jobs. Most of these mothers found the questions strange. Their children (again five to six years in age) were "still babies" (although they could be asked to help mind or amuse still younger children). The jobs belonged to the mother (as one mother said, "You don't have children just to give your jobs to them"). And there was little suggestion that early practice might have benefits ("She'll get lumbered with those jobs soon enough when she's married," said a mother) (Goodnow, Cashmore, Cotton, and Knight, 1984).

In similar fashion, explanations in terms of need turn out not to be sufficient. They fit well with reports of children doing more in large and in rural families than in small and urban families (White and Brinkerhoff, 1981). Accounts only in terms of need, however, do not fit well with reports to the effect that even child film stars are expected to do some household tasks (Zelizer, 1985). Need for help on the part of parents is now not a relevant factor. The expectation of work contributions seems instead to be offered as proof that the parents are behaving well: proof that the children, despite their status and their income, are being brought up as American children should be (Zelizer, 1985).

Accounts in terms of gender display similar problems. They offer a great deal in relation to differences in the work of sons and daughters but less with regard to the nature of conflict or negotiation. Accounts in terms of socialization into competence are also promising. Household competence, like all other forms of competence, can be seen as based on guided participation and, in association with changes of competence, linked to changes in the position people occupy within a social group (Lave and Wenger, 1991; Rogoff, Mistry, Goncu, and Mosier, 1993). Not well covered by this kind of account, however, are the expectations that lead to the selection of some tasks—but not others—as desirable areas of competence and to the presence of strong feelings about children performing more or less well.

The best course, it seems, is to start without commitments to any particular type of account. We shall instead first lay out the steps needed in order to develop a more satisfying picture and then see what emerges from taking those steps.

Some Baseline Steps and Proposals

We see three steps that are needed in order to develop a framework for thinking about family contributions, together with what we came to propose in relation to those steps.

• *Step 1: Moving toward an enriched description of contributions made or expected.* The characteristic that has attracted most attention to date is the quality of amount, expressed in either absolute or relative terms (for example, the number of hours I contribute or that number in relation to what others contribute). Amount is a quality that has a particular link to questions about the fairness of contributions. Descriptions in terms only of amount, however, fail to capture much of what is significant about contributions of any kind (Goodnow, 1998).

What other qualities of contributions might be considered? We have come to propose that contributions vary in a number of ways, with three important qualities being the style of a contribution, the extent to which it is person specific, and the degree of consensus, that is, the extent to which people follow the same pattern or share the same ideas about what should occur.

Style refers to the fact that contributions vary in the way they are made. They may, for example, be taken for granted rather than being reflected on, discussed, or seen as open to question. They vary also in the extent to which they are mandatory or optional, volunteered or made in response to reminders, undertaken with good grace or after resistance and negotiation.

Person specificity refers to the extent to which contributions are typically made by particular family members and are seen as fixed, movable to others, or open to substitutions.

Consensus refers to agreement among members of a family or a social group. It is the quality highlighted in analyses of conflict between parents and adolescents (for example, Montemayor, 1983) and in analyses of the several ways by which people within a family may come to differ from one another in the views they hold (from not hearing clearly what the other is advocating to hearing clearly but following another agenda: for example, Goodnow, 1996).

Paying attention to these several qualities, we propose, enriches our descriptions of what people do. It also helps specify the effects of various circumstances and the sources of strong feelings with regard to contributions made or not made.

• *Step 2: Considering the impact of various circumstances.* Circumstances range from the age, gender, competence, preferences, or family position of the individual to the ethnic background of the family or the spirit of the times. They include factors such as custom, parents' needs, or the availability of children who can help.

Rather than assume that any single circumstance—gender, for example—drives what is done or what is expected, we have come to propose that no single circumstance and no single process accounts for the nature of contributions. The better model appears to be of a multifactor kind. Need, availability, custom, and the effort required to get work done, for example, may all be factors that parents take into account when they consider the possibility of asking for a child's contribution. The first challenge, then, is to work out the circumstances to which people give most weight in the face of particular decisions or judgments about contributions.

We have also come to propose that circumstances may differentially affect one or more of the qualities of contributions. A change in age or status within the family, for example, may have weak effects on amount but strong effects on the style of a contribution. It may, for instance, alter the extent to which a contribution is taken for granted. Or it may change a contribution from being one that is made without negotiation and without payment to one that is now perceived as a matter for negotiation and possible payment. Alternately, a particular circumstance—an increase in a mother's need for help, for example—may alter the quality of amount but not the quality of person specificity. It may, for example, alter the amount that is expected of daughters but not of sons. The challenge lies in linking particular circumstances to particular qualities of contributions and in accounting for those links.

• *Step 3: Taking a closer look at the feelings people express about work contributions.* Why, for example, do parents often put considerable effort into seeing that their children make work contributions? Why do they often feel strongly about contributions made or avoided, or about the style with which a contribution was made?

We have come to propose that the significance of work contributions lies in their links to ideas about family membership, family status, and family relationships. To use the words of some of the parents interviewed, it is because "we are a family" that "you do your share," "you give others a hand," "you don't just look after yourself" (Goodnow, 1996). It is because people in families are meant to have some respect for each other and some concern for each other's feelings and interests, adolescents say, that "you don't act like it's the army," "you don't act as if they've nothing better to do," "you trust people to do their jobs," and "you don't treat other people as if they were your servants" ("you don't act like Lord Muck," to use an Australian expression) (Goodnow and Warton, 1992). There are undoubtedly other ways in which the obligations of family membership and position are taught or expressed, but work contributions clearly emerge as one of these.

These three steps and proposals are stated in bare-bones form. To place more flesh on the skeleton—to see how the steps and the proposals operate in practice—we turn to an illustrative series of studies that concentrate on one particular quality of work: its movability from one family member to another.

Contributions: Movable or Person Specific?

We have already proposed that work contributions may exhibit a number of qualities. Part of the reason that we focus on this is that within analyses of work contributions, it is standard practice to ask who typically does what and whether any current pattern is flexible or firm (one way of asking about its possible sources). Work contributions typically differ, for example, by gender. To that observation, however, we need to add questions about how far that differentiation holds and what might weaken it. Do gendered patterns break down, for example, when families contain only boys or only girls rather than both? In a sizable sample of urban Australian families containing children ten to fourteen years old, the answer was no (Antill, Goodnow, Cotton, and Russell, 1996). Availability alone, that result suggests, is not the influential factor. Any move away from traditional patterns may instead call for a combination of need and the unavailability of a traditional contributor.

Many comments on work, however, suggest that a further factor is involved. Certain jobs appear to belong to particular people. They are "men's work" or "women's work." They are described as "mine," "yours," or possibly "ours." They may then be seen as not properly handed over to others— "You don't have children just to give your jobs to them," to repeat the words of one mother, or "That's not my job" or "Not my problem" in the words of people of many ages when asked to take on a particular task. To accounts in terms of need and availability, it appears, we need to add ideas about ownership and the propriety of any movement of work from one person to another: ideas that may place limits on flexibility and account for some of the affect often attached to proposals for change.

To explore this aspect of contributions, we outline three approaches, together with a series of studies that illustrate how these approaches can be translated into practice and how the main results feed back into the baseline steps proposed (enriching the description of contributions, spelling out the circumstances that make a difference, and accounting for affect).

The three approaches start from these questions: What can you ask someone else to do? Who can be asked? What follows if people accept? They have now been used in research involving adult couples (Goodnow and Bowes, 1994) and adult siblings caring for an elderly parent in need of assistance (Goodnow, Lawrence, Karantzas, and Ryan, 2000; Lawrence, Goodnow, Karantzas, and Lin, 2000). Here, we limit the illustrative studies to people in the age range eight to eighteen.

Approach 1: What Can You Ask Someone Else to Do? In one application of this approach, mothers of nine to eleven year olds were asked how they felt about asking one child to do another child's usual job (these children all had siblings within two years of their age) (Goodnow and Delaney, 1989). In a second application, participants aged eight, eleven, and fourteen years were asked which tasks from a given set they could ask another member of the family to do for them on a busy day (Warton and Goodnow, 1991).

Enriching the Description of Contributions: The Nature of Distinctions. Both studies brought out the presence of distinctions among tasks in terms of their movability. The main distinction was between self-care and family-work tasks, with the former far less movable than the latter. *Self-care* covers all the activities to which one might attach the adjectives *yours* or *your own:* you make "your own bed," you put away "your own toys, your own clothes, the cup you just used," and so on. *Family work* covers activities that have some beneficial effects for others: for example, setting a table, helping prepare a meal, feeding the family cat or a dog, or taking out the trash.

Why the difference? The underlying principle emerged as one of causation: stated less formally, "your mess, your job" or "your stuff, your job." Beneath that distinction, there appears also a concern—at least among mothers—with the kind of relationship implied by expecting someone else to take over a self-care job. Mothers described themselves, for example, as often needing to point out that they should not be expected, once children were competent, to be forever picking up after those children. To use some of the mothers' phrases, "mothers are not maids," and the house is "a home, not a hotel [or restaurant, or laundromat, and so on]." That children make some of the same distinctions is suggested by their using phrases such as, "I'm not your slave." We have less evidence for children's relationship distinctions than we do for mothers'.

An underlying concern with who created the need for this work, we should add, is not the only basis for distinguishing among work contributions. To take a contrast example, we are currently finding that people in a variety of age groups (from ages eighteen to eighty) regard family members as having a particular responsibility to provide emotional support and companionship to an elderly parent in need of assistance. Assistance with housework or shopping may be farmed out to people outside the family, but the provision of emotional help is a family responsibility (Goodnow, Lawrence, Karantzas, and Ryan, 2000; Lawrence, Goodnow, Karantzas, and Lin, 2000).

Adding to What We Know About Circumstances. A circumstance that is always of particular interest is age. It turned out to have some provocative connections to the views held. Among the eight- to fourteen-year-old informants, for example, there was little variation in the view that self-care tasks are the ones you should try to do yourself rather than asking someone else. Adults in couple relationships also make the distinction (Goodnow and Bowes, 1994). So also, some data suggest, do children as young as age four. Children in the United States at least know that "if you both play, you should both clean up" (Shure, 1968). We might well begin to ask whether there is much room for an age effect on the way people regard this aspect of work contributions.

The area of impact appears to lie in the acceptance of exceptions to the rule. Mothers, for example, described themselves as making exceptions and sometimes asking one child to do another's self-care tasks. The justifications were in terms of helping everybody (for example, "We're all in a hurry to go out," or "We're a family; we all help each other") or in terms of reciprocity (for example, "They would do it for you") (Goodnow and Delaney, 1989).

Children were less prepared to make exceptions. Of the three age groups considered (eight, eleven, and fourteen years old), only the fourteen-year-old group contained a sizable percentage (40 percent as against 5 percent in the other two age groups) who said that it was fair for a parent to ask one child to clean up after two of them had played a game together. The justifications for fairness focused on reciprocity over time (for example, "It will even out in the long run" or "I'll see that they do it all next time") (Warton and Goodnow, 1991). At this age, then, the softening of the "your job—don't try to move it" principle appears to stem more from a recognition of the enduring quality of a family setting and of one's own capacity to make things even out than from some sense of family as a group where a strict concern with even contributions, or with who gave rise to the need for this work, may be inappropriate. At this point, we have still to learn at what age or under what circumstances adolescents or young adults move into this more communal (Clark and Chrisman, 1994) view of family relationships.

Helping to Account for Affect and the Significance of the Family Setting. The remarks on task distinctions and on circumstances already say something about the relevance of the family setting. Families are potentially places where its members can consider long-term balances and may put the good of others above the strict application of a rule such as "your mess [or your stuff], your job."

Families also emerge as settings that can invite ambiguity and tension with regard to expectations and principles. Few families provide detailed job descriptions. In fact, expectations may be fuzzy. The Anglo mothers interviewed, for instance, were in many ways teaching two principles: (1) the importance of people not expecting others to clean up after them and (2) the importance of doing more than looking after oneself and of setting the self-care rule aside for the sake of the family.

One source of differences between a parent's and a child's views may lie in the parents' message not being clear. In the long run, the hope appears to be that children will understand two principles. One is the importance of being responsible for what is theirs or for what they have directly caused. The other is the importance of doing more than that: the importance of being responsible for what affects others in the family. In the course of emphasizing the first principle, however, mothers may make the second less easy to establish (Goodnow, 2000).

In addition, the ways in which Anglo mothers proceed in practice may not best express the message they hope to convey. In practice, these mothers in the studies did in fact clean up after others. Most of the time, they did so routinely rather than in response to some exceptional circumstances. For many, the underlying hope seemed to be that their actions would be seen as having some of the qualities of a gift and not be taken for granted. Regularly given, however, gifts can easily come to be taken for granted, to be seen as simply what mothers do or as the receiver's right. In effect, the course of daily life may invite actions that do not fit well with the message one hopes to convey and create a degree of ambiguity that may easily become a source of tension.

Approach 2: Who Can Be Asked? It is one thing to establish that some contributions are more movable than others. We need next to ask who might pick up these contributions or might be expected to do so. As with the first approach (What can you ask someone else to do?), our data have to do with work contributions. The question, however, could be asked about any other kind of contribution.

The illustrative study is one in which eight, eleven, and fourteen year olds and their parents (mothers and fathers, in this case) were asked how they would feel about asking particular people to take on certain tasks (Goodnow and others, 1991).

The eight- to fourteen-year-old respondents were asked to imagine themselves in a family containing a father, a mother, a sister, and a brother and to give a yes or no answer to the question: "Could you ask ____ to do this job for you?" The tasks were make your bed, set the table, wash the car, and clean a bathtub or basin. The parents were provided with a set of seventeen tasks and asked, for each task, how they would feel about asking their partner, a teenage son, or a teenage daughter to do that task: "Would you ask with no second thoughts, think about it but ask, do it yourself (not ask), or have no need to ask (the job would be done)? And why would you choose one option rather than another?"

Enriching the Description of Contributions: Boundary Lines to Movability. Moving any contribution is likely to involve some sense of boundary lines. These are lines that are not crossed, with the net effect that involving some particular people is viewed as out of the question. Within analyses of household work contributions, gender is the boundary line most often considered, usually in the form of noting which tasks are seldom or never undertaken by males or females.

The results in our illustrative studies brought out the need to consider demarcation lines based on gender, generation, and ownership. Among the eight to fourteen year olds, for example, setting a table could cross gender lines (could go to a brother or a sister) but rarely moved across generation lines (rarely asked of a father or a mother). In contrast, washing a car or cleaning a bathroom rarely crossed gender lines. Washing a car could be asked of a father or brother but rarely of a mother or sister. The reverse was true for bathroom cleaning. Making a bed brought out ownership, with one additional feature: it was the task for which the majority of children said they would not ask anyone else to do. They would do it themselves or leave it undone. If they did ask another family member, however, the people nominated were mothers and sisters, for reasons that may have had to do with the perception that these were female tasks or that mothers and sisters might be more willing. On either basis, some boundary lines seem more permeable than others.

Adding to What We Know About Circumstances. Age is once more a circumstance of particular interest. Age might mean, for example, that the demarcation line of gender softened as children moved closer to adulthood. If anything, the reverse was the case (Goodnow and others, 1991). The fourteen year olds were less likely than the eight or eleven year olds to cross gender lines for the car and the bathroom tasks. The drop, however, applied only to siblings (the gendered distinctions between parents did not change). As siblings grew older, a whole new world for the possible movement of tasks and for applying gender schemas may be opening up. At the least, we clearly need to consider the family distribution of tasks as covering movement among siblings as well as movement between parents and children.

The results from parents brought out a further aspect of circumstances: the extent to which people often balance a number of considerations before making a request rather than making a request or an assignment on the basis of one circumstance alone. Gender was seldom mentioned explicitly. Instead, the considerations mentioned were a mixture of availability, competence, preferences (for example, "He quite likes to cook"), and resistance ("All I'd get on that one is a lot of argument"). From one parent to another, variations occurred in the degree of emphasis given to particular circumstances. Future research might well move toward specifying how the weights attached to particular circumstances vary from family member to family member or from time to time.

Helping to Account for Affect and the Significance of the Family Setting. The main new point to emerge was the need to consider what family relationships implied for the ways in which requests should be made. The mothers in this group, for example, were comfortable with questions phrased in terms of asking either a partner or a teenage son or daughter. A number of fathers in this group, however, expressed surprise at the notion of "asking" rather than "telling" (Goodnow and others, 1991).

What matters, it appears, is not only what is asked for but also a particular aspect of style: in this case, the procedures used in relation to a request (Goodnow, 1998). To expand on that point, we add a result from a separate study: one involving adults in couple relationships (Goodnow and Bowes, 1994). Couple relationships, it turned out, carry implications not only for the style of requests but also for the way in which requests are declined. It is one thing to decline on the grounds of being incompetent, unavailable at the time needed, or perhaps already overcontributing ("I've done that three times this week already," for example). To be unwilling is another, presenting the family member who does not wish to take on a task with the challenge of finding acceptable ways to say no or to make it unlikely that he or she will be asked in the first place.

Approach 3: What Follows If People Accept? Movability does not end with a request and an acceptance. Suppose, for example, that you have asked another person to take on a particular job, to make a particular contribution. Should you check that this actually happens? If so, how should you check? Who should be blamed if the contribution is not made?

Again, these are questions that can be asked in relation to any contribution, any setting, and any age group. Within analyses of blame and courtroom settings, for example, these are known as questions about direct and indirect responsibility (Rawls, 1972). They are also opportunities to learn more about the possible movement of tasks among siblings (as against their movement across generations) and to gain a further sense of whether and how relationships matter. The informants in the illustrative studies were fourteen and eighteen year olds (Goodnow and Warton, 1992, 1996).

Enriching the Description of Contributions: Obligations Continue. In both of the age groups, the large majority agreed that the asker had the obligation to check that the job was done and that some degree of blame could be assigned to both parties if the job was not done. There were outliers in both groups—people who insisted that the original owner's responsibility ended once someone else had agreed to do the job—but this judgment was not related to either age or gender. Overall, an agreement to make a requested contribution—a pledge—is clearly not the end of the story.

Adding to What We Know About Circumstances. Within the illustrative studies so far, the gender of the person expressing a viewpoint has not made a significant difference. That was not the case in the part of the delegation results that had to do with preferred and possible methods of checking that a job had been done.

In one procedure, three methods were described for checking on a job: people watching while you work, pointing out bits before you have finished, and checking but pretending that they are not. The majority disliked all of these. The third method, however, was less disliked than the others, on the grounds that it helped avoid the other person's being "embarrassed" or "offended" or the appearance of not trusting the other (in the words of several, "You should be able to trust your family"). A clear gender difference also appeared in relation to the extent to which the third method was disliked: males found disguised checking more objectionable than did females.

In a second procedure, eighteen year olds who had some part-time paid work were asked whether arrangements were different at home and in paid work. Again, a gender difference emerged. All of the males regarded the two settings as unequivocally different, with most of the differences having to do with degrees of choice and openness—for example, "In a family, there's more trust and openness; in a workplace there's more of a hierarchy, and when you're expected to do something, you've got to do it" (Goodnow and Warton, 1992, p. 102). In contrast, only 47 percent of the females regarded the two settings as unequivocally different, with relationships still a significant issue—for example, "If it's a closely knit working group, it should be like a family" (Goodnow and Warton, 1992, p. 103). Whether the nature of paid work is different for young men and women or whether their perceptions of what should happen in the two settings is different is an open issue. On either basis, however, gender emerged as an influence on the links drawn between a way of working and the nature of relationships.

Helping to Account for Affect and the Significance of the Family Setting. The delegation studies provoke some new questions about perceptions of the family setting: What settings are seen as different from the family? And who draws what distinctions? The gender difference just noted above, for example, makes one wonder who is especially likely to draw sharp distinctions between family and not family, between home as a place of trust and warmth and work as a "jungle."

The delegation studies also brought out a further way in which the family setting can be a source of tension. The fourteen and eighteen year olds were asked to describe ways of being reminded that they liked and disliked (Goodnow and Warton, 1992). (They had all agreed that the asker had the obligation to give a reminder if it appeared that the task might not be done.) The disliked ways were frequently ways that implied the task taker "was not going to get to it," when in fact he or she "was going to get to it" but "after I've finished what I'm doing" or perhaps "in my own good time."

In contrast, the liked ways were forms of reminding that displayed "respect," that implied "we are equals." These were, for example, reminders in the form of asking nicely "whether you'd had a chance to get to it yet." Issues of control, autonomy, and status are clearly at stake, calling for some delicacy when it comes to ways of asking for work contributions and responding to those requests.

What Happens in Other Cultural Groups? There is still a great deal to be learned about the movability of various family contributions. One direction that seems especially relevant to the development of a general framework, however, has to do with the possibility that all we have learned so far is specific to Anglo families.

One step in that direction comes by way of a study comparing adolescents in several countries (Bowes, Flanagan, and Taylor, 2001). Presented with a variety of reasons for contributions of household work, adolescents in Australia and the United States chose "the development of a sense of responsibility" more often than they chose "benefits to the family." The reverse frequency pattern held for adolescents in Czechoslovakia, Hungary, and Sweden. The expressed ideology with regard to contributions apparently varies even among industrialized Western countries.

A second step toward exploring cultural effects is contained in a study with mothers in Beijing by Bowes, Chen, Li, and Li (1999). The core questions revolved around a situation in which a child is asked to put away all of the materials left on a table after the child and a friend have played together. (The prevalence of one-child families made the second child a friend rather than a sibling.)

Chinese mothers turned out to endorse the notion that children should learn to put away their own things and to clean up after their projects. They did not, however, expect much negotiation in relation to their request, and they held views about negotiation that were not Anglo in style. Replies in the form of, "I didn't use all those things," for example, were not acceptable (they were also regarded as not frequent). Replies in the form of, "Later, after I've done my homework," were regarded as reasonable and more frequent. Mothers also described themselves as not likely to insist on a task being done if a child seemed reluctant, with a preference given to maintaining harmony and avoiding requests that might bring about a confrontation.

Left unanswered for the moment is the question of whether in Chinese society, these approaches to contributions and to negotiations are specific to parent-child relationships. Among classmates assigned the task of cleaning up a classroom, objections and negotiations along the lines of "not my job" or "not my stuff" are said to be more frequent (M. J. Chen, personal communication, 1999). Objections and negotiations might also be more frequent among siblings. That possibility cannot be pursued in China. In other cultural groups, however, it would clearly be worthwhile breaking ideas about assistance, obligation, and negotiation in the family setting into those that apply to parent-child relationships and those that apply to sibling relationships. The obligations that go with family relationships—the help one might be expected to give and the ways in which this is worked out—may be quite different in relation to parents and to siblings. That distinction may become all the more important as two or more children reach an age where direct negotiations with one another about work contributions, that is, without going through parents, become more likely.

Conclusion

From among the several directions that expansions might take, we chose one that is particularly appropriate to this volume. What does the kind of framework outlined suggest with regard to a particular age period: in this case, adolescence and early adulthood? What might be specific about work contributions to the family at this part of the life span?

The possibilities we suggest rest on two arguments. One is that household work contributions are often vehicles for working out larger issues. They provide a concrete practice that can be pointed to, discussed, and used as a way of negotiating change on occasions where more abstract wishes and objections—issues of respect, justice, being treated like an adult, and making one's own decisions—are often difficult to articulate or to be understood in the same ways by various family members. As with many other practices, it is these embodied meanings that are at the heart of satisfaction or discontent, of pressures for change and resistance to change (Goodnow, Miller, and Kessel, 1995).

The other underlying argument is that for any age period, what matters most is the combination of features of the individual and of the setting in which contributions are to be made.

The period before being fully regarded as an adult, for example, is a time of change for the individual. There are changes in competence, in the status that is wished for, and in agendas or competing activities. Each of these changes is likely to have flow-on effects of various kinds.

Changes in competence, for example, make it likely that there will be a shift in what others expect to be contributed. Changes in competence should also make it easier for the adolescent to understand subtleties in the application of a rule and to engage in more complex forms of negotiation or resistance.

Changes in the status that is wished for are likely to have effects of several kinds. They may affect first of all the kinds of comparisons made with others in the family. We may now expect, for example, more frequent comparisons not only with siblings but also with same-sex adults in the family, checking in each case what they do or are expected to do (McHale, Bartko, Crouter, and Perry-Jenkins, 1990). In addition, household work increasingly may be claimed as an area for discretionary judgment as to when and how well a task should be carried out ("In my own good time," to repeat one adolescent's phrase). Adolescence, for example, certainly brings an increasing tendency to regard the state of one's room as an area where adolescents rather than parents should make the rules (Smetana, 1989).

The wish for adult status is also likely to bring with it an increased sensitivity to the style with which a request is made or a reminder given. That sensitivity certainly appeared in the delegation study (Goodnow and Warton, 1992). It is highlighted also, to take some informal examples, by a parent's report of being asked by a fourteen year old, "Is this a request or an order?" and by a fifteen year old's objection to her father's approach to work contributions: "I don't mind doing the work, but he insists that I have to do it cheerfully. He says, every time, `If you can't do it with a good grace, I'd rather you didn't do it at all.' I don't even have the right to grumble."

What effects might flow on from the third change, an increasing involvement in activities outside the family (for example, activities with peers or involvement in paid work)? Paid work provides an especially interesting circumstance. It offers access to one's own money and an implied adult status. It offers experience with the way things are done outside the family setting, providing a contrast case and possibly the occasion to recognize that families are in a special category when it comes to work contributions. Like all other forms of outside involvement, paid work also makes it more likely that the young person's own agenda becomes a weightier circumstance to consider, competing with the priorities that parents may have in mind.

Finally, paid work seems likely to lead people to wonder, Where do work contributions at home fit into my probable future? In a study by Straus

(1962), for example, the boys most satisfied with the work contributions they made at home were boys working on farms, although they put in longer hours and were paid less than boys of the same age in town. The boys on the farm, however, saw the work they did as relevant to their future as farmers. The town boys saw the work they did as irrelevant to what they expected to become.

All of these changes seem likely to prompt adolescents to question what they do and to become interested in change. Those features of adolescence, however, always need to be considered in terms of how they mesh with features of the family setting. The features we select for attention are the fuzziness of expectations, the tolerance of various ways of proceeding, and the degree of openness to change.

The family is a setting where there may often be a certain fuzziness to expectations, and that fuzziness might be confusing for young children. Adolescents, in contrast, may find fuzziness easier to accept once their own ability to understand subtlety increases or once they recognize that fuzziness could be to their advantage when it comes to working toward change.

Families differ also in the extent to which they tolerate or approve of various ways of proceeding. Their visions of the future, for example, may make it easy or difficult to live with an imbalance in contributions: to be comfortable, for instance, with the idea that work contributions will be drastically reduced during a tough year in school and perhaps redressed at a later time (or not redressed at all). Concepts of negotiation may also vary across generations and among families, making an acceptable style all the more important. It is, for example, the style with which adolescents present their case for more control over rules that, in Smetana's (1988) study, makes the difference between an expression of opinion being regarded by parents as a difference rather than a conflict.

Families may also contain varying degrees of room for change. Room for change may depend on the extent to which there are other people available to whom a job may be moved. Wishes for change, for example, count for little if the work has to be done and there is no other person in the family to take it over (a basis, it would seem, for arguments about the extent to which various forms of household work are really necessary and might be dropped altogether). Room for a change in status also affects the fate of an adolescent's preferences. Families vary, for example, in the extent to which they are marked by hierarchical patterns. A hierarchical pattern might apply to all interactions: mother-child, father-child, and older-younger siblings. That solid wall might well make negotiations difficult. Differences among these patterns, however, open up the possibility of working for change in one relationship at a time: change in the way a mother expects or assigns work, for example, before change with regard to a father. Arrangements with siblings, especially when they are of an age when work can be traded back and forth without a parent's being involved, may be even more likely to be the first sites for negotiation and change.

Finally, families are themselves often in the process of change, especially with regard to what is needed, when, and how much negotiation is tolerable. It would be unproductive to think only in terms of adolescents pushing for change while family members and family relationships remain static or resistant. There may well be occasions of lag, of persistence in old images and old expectations. Changes, however, often occur. Expectations about work, in fact, may change from year to year or even over the course of a week (weekdays contrasted with weekends, for example).

Here, then, is a point in the family life cycle where, for a variety of particular reasons, the expectations and needs of several family members may or may not mesh well. In an ideal world, both parties may seek change in the same direction, in circumstances that make change feasible. In practice, one party but not the other may seek change, or both may seek change but not in the same direction. The pivotal factor will always be the combination of people and their settings.

Would the same kinds of people-in-contexts analysis not also apply to every age period? The answer is yes. What is likely to vary, however, is the nature of the circumstances that give rise to an easy or a difficult combination. To take old age as a contrast case, the individual is again in a position of change with regard to the contributions that can be made to the care of oneself and of others. The changes on this occasion, however, may be unwanted, not readily acknowledged to oneself, a source of worry to others, and a possible occasion for the loss rather than the gain of autonomy and control. What matters, nonetheless, is the extent to which those changes coincide with some particular characteristics of other family members: their ability and willingness, for example, to take on new obligations, negotiate change, and do so in ways that help maintain images of competence and status for all involved.

In effect, the particular qualities of contributions, the impact of particular circumstances, and the particular significance of contributions for affect and family relationships may vary from one age period to another. Attention to each of these elements of a general framework can help the analysis of any particular part of the family cycle and any cultural or historical context.

References

Antill, J., Goodnow, J. J., Russell, G., and Cotton, S. "Gendered Patterns of Household Work: Effects of Family Composition." *Sex Roles*, 1996, *34*, 215–236.

Berk, S. F. *The Gender Factory*. New York: Plenum Press, 1985.

Bowes, J. M., Chen, M. J., Li, Q. S., and Li, Y. "Asking Children to Help: Culturally Acceptable Justifications." *Journal for Australian Research in Early Childhood*, 1999, *6*, 9–17.

Bowes, J. M., Flanagan, C., and Taylor, A. J. "Adolescents' Ideas About Individual and Social Responsibility in Relation to Children's Household Work: Some International Comparisons." *International Journal of Behavioral Development*, 2001, *25*, 60–68.

Clark, M. S., and Chrisman, K. "Resource Allocation in Intimate Relationships: Trying to Make Sense of a Confusing Literature." In M. J. Lerner and G. Mikula (eds.), *Entitlement and the Affectional Bond.* New York: Plenum Press, 1994.

Goodnow, J. J. "Children's Household Work: Its Nature and Functions." *Psychological Bulletin,* 1988, *103,* 5–26.

Goodnow, J. J. "From Household Practices to Parents' Ideas About Work and Interpersonal Relationships." In S. Harkness and C. Super (eds.), *Parents' Cultural Belief Systems.* New York: Guilford Press, 1996.

Goodnow, J. J. "Beyond the Overall Balance: The Significance of Particular Tasks and Procedures for Perceptions of Fairness in Distributions of Household Work." *Social Justice Research,* 1998, *11,* 359–376.

Goodnow, J. J. "On Being Responsible for More Than You Have Actually Caused." In W. van Haaften, T. Wren, and A. Tellings (eds.), *Moral Sensibilities and Education.* Bemmel, Netherlands: Concorde, 2000.

Goodnow, J. J., and Bowes, J. M. *Men, Women, and Household Work.* New York: Oxford University Press, 1994.

Goodnow, J. J., Bowes, J. M., Warton, D. M., Dawes, L. J., and Taylor, A. J. "Would You Ask Someone Else to Do This Task? Parents' and Children's Ideas About Household Work Requests." *Developmental Psychology,* 1991, *27,* 817–828.

Goodnow, J. J., Cashmore, J., Cotton, S., and Knight, R. "Mothers' Developmental Timetables in Two Cultural Groups." *International Journal of Psychology,* 1984, *19,* 193–205.

Goodnow, J. J., and Delaney, S. "Children's Household Work: Task Differences, Styles of Assignment, and Links to Family Relationships." *Journal of Applied Developmental Psychology,* 1989, *10,* 209–226.

Goodnow, J. J., Lawrence, J. A., Karantzas, G., and Ryan, J. "Caregiving: A Way to Explore Distributed Tasks and Shared Understandings." Unpublished manuscript, Macquarie University, Sydney, Australia, 2000.

Goodnow, J. J., Miller, P. J., and Kessel, F. (eds.). *Cultural Practices as Contexts for Development.* New Directions for Child Development, no. 67. San Francisco: Jossey-Bass, 1995.

Goodnow, J. J., and Warton, P. M. "Understanding Responsibility: Adolescents' Views of Delegation and Follow-Through Within the Family." *Social Development,* 1992, *1,* 89–106.

Goodnow, J. J., and Warton, P. M. "Direct and Indirect Responsibility: Distributing Blame." *Journal of Moral Education,* 1996, *25,* 37–49.

Grusec, J. E., Goodnow, J. J., and Cohen, L. "Household Work and the Development of Concern for Others." *Developmental Psychology,* 1996, *32,* 999–1007.

Lave, J., and Wenger, E. *Situated Learning: Legitimate Peripheral Participation.* Cambridge, England: Cambridge University Press, 1991.

Lawrence, J. A., Goodnow, J. J., Karantzas, G., and Lin, S-H. "Distributing Caregiving Tasks Among Siblings." Unpublished manuscript, University of Melbourne, Melbourne, Australia, 2000.

McHale, S. M., Bartko, T., Crouter, A. C., and Perry-Jenkins, M. "Children's Housework and Their Psychosocial Functioning: The Mediating Effects of Parents' Sex Role Behaviors and Attitudes." *Child Development,* 1990, *61,* 1413–1426.

Montemayor, R. "Parents and Adolescents in Conflict: All Families Some of the Time and Some Families All of the Time." *Journal of Early Adolescence,* 1983, *3,* 83-103.

Rawls, H. *A Theory of Justice.* New York: Oxford University Press, 1972.

Rheingold, H. L. "Little Children's Participation in the Work of Adults: A Nascent Prosocial Behavior." *Child Development,* 1982, *53,* 114–125.

Rogoff, B., Mistry, J., Goncu, A., and Mosier, C. "Guided Participation in Cultural Activity by Toddlers and Caregivers." *Monographs of the Society for Research in Child Development,* 1993, *58* (entire issue).

Shure, M. B. "Fairness, Generosity, and Selfishness: The Naive Psychology of Children and Adults." *Child Development,* 1968, *39,* 875–886.

Smetana, J. "Adolescents' and Parents' Conceptions of Parental Authority." *Child Development,* 1988, *59,* 321–325.

Smetana, J. "Adolescents' and Parents' Reasoning About Actual Family Conflict." *Child Development,* 1989, *60,* 1052–1067.

Staub, E. *Positive Prosocial Behavior and Morality.* Orlando, Fla.: Academic Press, 1979.

Straus, J. A. "Work Rules and Financial Responsibility in the Socialization of Farm, Fringe, and Town Boys." *Rural Sociology,* 1962, *27,* 257–274.

Warton, P. M., and Goodnow, J. J. "The Nature of Responsibility: Children's Understanding of 'Your Job.'" *Child Development,* 1991, *62,* 156–165.

White, L. K., and Brinkerhoff, D. B. "Children's Work in the Family: Its Significance and Meaning." *Journal of Marriage and the Family,* 1981, *43,* 789–798.

Zelizer, V. *Pricing the Priceless Child.* New York: Basic Books, 1985.

JACQUELINE J. GOODNOW is a professorial research fellow in the Department of Psychology, Macquarie University, Sydney, Australia.

JEANETTE A. LAWRENCE is associate professor in the Department of Psychology, University of Melbourne, Australia.

2

Early research on working mothers suggested that girls took on more housework when their mothers were employed outside the home. This chapter takes an updated look at this issue by asking whether daughters take on more housework when their mothers report stressful occupational conditions and by making within-family comparisons of sons' versus daughters' involvement in housework.

Household Chores: Under What Conditions Do Mothers Lean on Daughters?

Ann C. Crouter, Melissa R. Head, Matthew F. Bumpus, Susan M. McHale

Household chores are a routine part of children's daily activities in many cultures (Goodnow, 1988; Larson and Verma, 1999; Whiting and Whiting, 1975). Although there is a vast literature on the correlates of the division of labor for husbands and wives (for example, Coltrane, 2000), much less is known about the conditions underlying children's and adolescents' involvement in household chores in contemporary American families.

One correlate of children's involvement in housework that has received considerable attention is gender. Indeed, in their recent review of children's and adolescents' use of time around the world, Larson and Verma (1999) concluded, "Across nearly all populations—regardless of economic development or schooling—girls spend more time in household labor than do boys" (p. 707). They also noted that the one exception to this rule may be the United States today. Although gender differences in American children's

We gratefully acknowledge the assistance of Alan Booth, Devon Corneal, Jacinda Dariotis, Maria Eguia, Heather Helms-Erikson, Julia Jackson-Newsom, Mary Maguire, Corinna Jenkins Tucker, and Kimberly Updegraff and feedback from Andrew Fuligni and Tom Weisner. This research, which was supported by grant R01-HD32336-02 from the National Institute of Child Health and Human Development as part of the Middle Childhood Initiative (Ann C. Crouter and Susan M. McHale, Co-Principal Investigators), was first presented at the biennial meeting of the Society for Research on Adolescence, Chicago, April 2000.

housework performance were routinely found in research in the 1980s (Medrich, Roizen, Rubin, and Buckley, 1982; White and Brinkerhoff, 1981), the recent literature presents contradictory findings. Some studies have found that girls do more housework than boys do; others have not found this (see Larson and Verma, 1999).

The contradictory findings in this area may stem from the fact that sex-typed socialization in the area of household task performance occurs more in some family contexts than it does in others (see Crouter, Manke, and McHale, 1995). What are the relevant contextual dimensions? Simply having a brother versus a sister may determine how involved a given child is in housework. Medrich, Roizen, Rubin, and Buckley (1982), in their study of sixth-grade children's time use, noted that "the presence of an older sister . . . lightened the load of a sixth-grade boy but not of a sixth-grade girl," adding that "such differences were probably less the results of deliberate and conscious decisions on the part of parents than of unconscious and habitual patterns of socialization, at least as far as sex was concerned" (p. 145). Another relevant dimension of the family context is parents' employment. Medrich, Roizen, Rubin, and Buckley (1982), for example, found that "when the mother worked it was more likely to increase a daughter's than a son's chore responsibilities" (p. 144).

In this chapter, we focus on some of the conditions that may give rise to differences in boys' and girls' involvement in household work. Unlike previous work in this area, we employed a sibling design to study gender differences. Specifically, we compared levels of involvement in housework for two siblings in each family by exploring the implications of the sex composition of the sibling dyad and the parents' work situations for involvement in housework in a sample of dual-earner families with school-age children. Interested in whether the sibling division of labor served as a socialization context for children's attitudes about gender, we also examined whether the siblings' division of labor was connected to children's attitudes about gender roles.

Parents' Employment and Children's Participation in Housework

Early research in the maternal employment tradition suggested that mothers' work status was an important determinant of children's involvement in housework (Medrich, Roizen, Rubin, and Buckley, 1982; White and Brinkerhoff, 1981). Ironically, although dual-earner families are often conceptualized as less sex-typed family environments than father breadwinner–mother homemaker families, because employment has been considered a nontraditional role for women, early research suggested that when mothers worked outside the home, their daughters actually took on a greater share of household work in comparison to other daughters and in comparison to the sons of employed mothers. In White and Brinkerhoff's (1981) words, girls with employed mothers "sink . . . even further into the domestic role" (p. 177).

One reason girls may become more involved in housework when their mothers hold paid jobs is that mothers typically perform the largest share of household work in families, and busy employed mothers may need help and turn to their daughters for support. Indeed, in an earlier study of first-born school-age children and their families, we found that although fathers typically performed more housework than their eldest children did, those fathers who performed less household work than their eldest offspring were three times more likely to have a firstborn daughter than a firstborn son (Manke, Seery, Crouter, and McHale, 1994). This suggests that some daughters may perform housework that fathers would ordinarily do and that in some families, girls handle an important share of the daily tasks that make families run smoothly.

Contemporary research on work and family has moved well beyond a preoccupation with employment status differences, as in the working mother–homemaker comparison, to a focus on the nature of parents' work (Parcel and Menaghan, 1994; Perry-Jenkins, Repetti, and Crouter, 2000). Researchers in this area are interested in how mothers' and fathers' occupational conditions, coupled with family circumstances, make their mark on children's activities and psychosocial functioning. In the analyses we present here, we are interested in those occupational and family conditions that may give rise to inequality between boys and girls in the allocation of housework. We reasoned that mothers may be particularly likely to lean on daughters—that is, to depend on daughters for help with household tasks—when mothers are employed in demanding, time-consuming jobs that make them feel pressured and overloaded. Evidence for this possible situation comes from Manke, Seery, Crouter, and McHale (1994), who found the most pronounced boy-girl differences in levels of participation in traditionally female-typed household tasks in families in which mothers were employed full time, as compared to families in which mothers were employed part time or were homemakers.

Within-Family and Between-Family Comparisons. The research design that Manke, Seery, Crouter, and McHale (1994) used was not optimal; like so many other studies of children in the family context, they focused on only one child in each family and were thus limited to making between-family comparisons of unrelated girls and boys. If parents have a tendency to assign household tasks on the basis of gender, however, or if children have a tendency to take on responsibility for household chores as a function of gender, these gender-based activity patterns should be most obvious in families containing both a son and a daughter (Crouter, Manke, and McHale, 1995; McHale, Crouter, and Tucker, 1999). In order to capture such within-family differences, a study must pay equal attention to at least two children in each family. In the research presented here, we have built within-family comparisons into our design by paying equal attention to the activities of the two eldest children in each family and by including roughly equal numbers of the four possible sibling gender combinations:

older sister–younger sister, older sister–younger brother, older brother–younger sister, and older brother–younger brother dyads.

Why Might Mothers Turn to Daughters and Not to Sons? Faced with a choice, the busy mother in demanding work circumstances may turn to a daughter rather than a son for several reasons. First, housework is a scripted part of women's roles in our society (Coltrane, 2000; Ferree, 1990; West and Zimmerman, 1987). Perhaps precisely because household tasks are so frequently equated with "women's work," many men and, presumably, boys resist participating in this domain of family life (Goode, 1982). For all of these reasons, it may feel natural for mothers to turn to daughters in the housework domain (Ferree, 1990). Second, the mother-daughter relationship tends to be a close one, and daughters tend to identify with mothers (Starrels, 1994). These relationship dynamics may encourage daughters to participate in their mothers' household activities and to be predisposed to be helpful when times are busy and stressful for their mothers. Indeed, some daughters may equate household work with providing love and care to family members, as some women have been found to do (DeVault, 1991). Finally, busy mothers may simply not have the time, energy, or inclination to cajole resistant sons into taking on household responsibilities even if mothers believe that males and females should take equal responsibility for these tasks (Manke, Seery, Crouter, and McHale, 1994). The tendency to turn to a daughter for help should be clearest in families with a son and a daughter (Medrich, Roizen, Rubin, and Buckley, 1982). If daughters are assigned to (or volunteer for) more tasks than their brothers, the gulf between them should be more pronounced than it would be for siblings who share the same gender. The tendency for a daughter to shoulder a disproportionate share of housework responsibility may be less apparent in families with two daughters than in those with a daughter and a son because when there are two daughters, mothers may spread out the work assignments across the two girls, or both daughters may step in to help.

Opposite-sex sibling dyads come in two forms: older sister–younger brother dyads and older brother–younger sister dyads. In late-middle childhood, the developmental period we focus on, the tendency for girls to do more housework than their brothers should be more pronounced in older sister–younger brother dyads than in older brother–younger sister pairs because two forces are conspiring to encourage older sisters' greater involvement in household chores: their greater relative age and associated maturity and their gender. Older brother–younger sister dyads, in contrast, represent an interesting situation. On the one hand, the boy should shoulder a heavier share of household tasks because he is older. On the other hand, if household activities fall along gender lines, the younger girl may do as much as, or even more than, her older brother because she is a girl. Finding that girls in older brother–younger sister dyads do a large share of housework in families in which mothers have demanding work circumstances would suggest that mothers lean on daughters (or that daughters step in to help) even when there is an older male sibling who presumably is more developmentally advanced.

The Sibling Division of Household Labor and Attitudes About Gender Roles: Is There a Connection? We are also interested in exploring the connections between the ways in which siblings divide housework and their attitudes about gender roles. At least for boys and girls growing up with a sibling of the other sex, the division of labor between the two siblings may send a message about gender roles that becomes incorporated into children's conceptualizations about gender. Alternatively, of course, siblings' attitudes may shape their participation in household tasks; if boys with traditional attitudes resist doing housework, for example, their attitudes may shape the siblings' division of labor rather than the other way around. We examined this issue cross-sectionally and longitudinally, recognizing that we cannot pin down causal relationships without an experimental design.

The Penn State Family Relationships Project

In this study, we examined one facet of how dual-earner families may function as settings for gender socialization by studying three issues.

First, moving beyond work status to consider how parents' occupational circumstances may give rise to the patterning of boys' and girls' involvement in housework, we hypothesized that when mothers experience heavy job demands, they lean on daughters for help.

Second, making both between-family comparisons of girls versus boys and within-family comparisons of sisters versus brothers, we hypothesized that the tendency for daughters to perform more housework would be most apparent in families with both a son and a daughter (that is, older sister–younger brother dyads and older brother–younger sister dyads). We anticipated that the girl-boy gap would be most dramatic in older sister–younger brother families because firstborn girls have gender and greater maturity pushing them in the direction of household task participation. We were also quite interested, however, in older brother–younger sister dyads because if girls do more housework in this situation, it would be strong evidence that busy mothers lean on daughters (or that their daughters step in to help).

Third, we examined the connections between sisters' and brothers' relative involvement in housework and their gender role attitudes. We explored this possible association only in families with both a son and daughter because household task assignments in such families offer a possible context for learning about gender. In families with two daughters or two sons, this is not the case. Here we tested no specific hypothesis. We examined this issue with cross-sectional data from Year 1 and longitudinal analyses examining relative change (in attitudes or behavior) from Year 1 to Year 3.

Overview of Methods. Participating families were recruited from eighteen school districts in central Pennsylvania. We sought two-parent, nondivorced families in which the eldest child was initially in the fourth or fifth grade and in which there was at least one sibling one to three years younger. We also sought families in which both parents were employed at least part time, although this was not a criterion for participation. Although most of the analyses reported here were based on data from Year 1, we also analyzed longitudinal data using Year 1 participation in housework and attitudes about gender to predict change in housework or attitudes from Year 1 to Year 3. Thus, the analyses presented here are based on data from the 172 dual-earner families for whom we have complete data at the two times of measurement. Reflecting the population of the small cities, towns, and rural communities in which families resided, the sample was predominantly white and working and middle class (see Table 2.1).

Data were collected using two procedures. First, mothers, fathers, firstborn ($M = 10.88$ years) and second-born ($M = 8.25$ years) preadolescent offspring were interviewed individually in their homes. Parents completed a variety of measures, including several instruments focused on work demands, and the preadolescents reported their gender role attitudes. Second, in a series of seven evening telephone interviews, held about an hour before the children went to bed, siblings reported (separately) on their daily activities, including their involvement in each of eleven household chores (for example, meal preparation, yard work, errands, laundry). These reports were aggregated to create indexes of total time spent on

Table 2.1. Means and Standard Deviations for Sample Demographic Characteristics at Year 1

	Mean	SD
Age		
Mothers	36.70	3.69
Fathers	38.99	5.01
Firstborns	10.88	0.56
Second-borns	8.25	0.92
Education (years)		
Mothers	14.64	2.12
Fathers	14.66	2.40
Firstborns	4.76	0.55
Second-borns	2.07	0.97
Work hours (per week)		
Mothers	33.97	14.43
Fathers	50.61	11.98
Income (dollars per year)		
Mothers	19,602	14,825
Fathers	40,317	23,334
Family size	4.53	0.74
Marriage duration (years)	13.63	2.46

housework (reported in minutes aggregated across the seven occasions of measurement). In earlier studies, we correlated family members' reports of joint activities as a way to check inter-rater reliability (Crouter, Maguire, Helms-Erikson, and McHale, 1999); we also used test-retest procedures by repeating certain questions at the end of each telephone call (McHale, Crouter, and Bartko, 1992). On the basis of these checks, we have concluded that this modified version of a daily diary procedure produces reliable data. On average, the firstborn girls in this study spent an average of 253 minutes across the seven days on the eleven household chores we asked about (SD = 141); the mean for firstborn boys was 273 minutes across the seven daily interviews (SD = 221.4). The means for second-born siblings were 233.3 minutes (SD = 201.5) and 194.8 minutes (SD = 153.9) across the seven days, for girls and boys, respectively.

During the home interview, mothers and fathers reported on a wide variety of issues, including three aspects of work demands:

Work hours, assessed by summing the number of hours per week parents report (1) spending at work, (2) working on job-related matters at home, and (3) commuting to and from work.

Work pressure, measured with the nine-item Work Pressure subscale of the Work Environment Scale (Moos, 1986). This measure taps the extent to which the job presents a fast pace and pressing deadlines (an example question is, "It is very hard to keep up with your workload"). In our sample, Cronbach's alpha was .79 for mothers and .72 for fathers.

Role overload, that is, the sense that parents feel busy, rushed, and overwhelmed by multiple commitments and demands. This was measured with the thirteen-item Role Overload Scale (Reilly, 1982). A sample item is, "There are too many demands on my time." Cronbach's alpha was .88 for mothers and .89 for fathers.

Children's gender role attitudes were assessed with the Children's Attitudes Towards Women Scale (Antill, Cotton, Goodnow, and Russell, 1994), which has nineteen items, each answered on a 4-point scale (for example, "Sons in a family should be given more help to go to college than daughters"). Scores can range from 19 to 76, with high scores reflecting more traditional attitudes. Cronbach's alpha was .83 for firstborns and .80 for second-borns.

Do Girls Take on More Housework When Mothers Experience Work Stress? To operationalize parental work demands, we used a typology previously developed by Bumpus, Crouter, and McHale (1999). They performed cluster analysis on fathers' and mothers' reports of work hours, pressure, and role overload with the goal of developing a typology of dual-earner families defined by the dyadic patterning of fathers' and mothers' work demands. This analysis revealed three groups: (1) a high-mother-demands group (*n* = 54 families), (2) a low-parental-demands group (*n* = 66 families), and (3) a high-father-demands group ($n = 52$ families; see Figure 2.1). In the high-mother-demands group, the mothers' level of work demands was high compared to that of other mothers and also compared to their own husband's. Similarly, fathers in the high-father-demands group reported higher work demands than other fathers and in comparison to their own wives. Both mothers and fathers in the low-demands group reported low levels of work demands. A central question for this chapter is whether the patterning of sons' versus daughters' involvement in housework differs in the high-mother-demands group compared to the other two groups.

A 3 (work group) × 2 (firstborn gender) × 2 (second-born gender) × 2 (sibling) mixed-model ANOVA, treating work group and the two siblings' genders as between-group factors, sibling as a within-group factor, and children's total time in housework as the dependent variable, revealed the predicted four-way interaction, $F(2, 160) = 3.26$, $p < .05$. To follow up this finding, we conducted Tukey tests on the sibling difference scores (the firstborn's time spent in housework minus the younger sibling's time spent in housework). Specifically, we compared the sibling difference scores of the four sibling gender constellations (older sister–younger sister, older sister–younger brother, and so on) separately for each of the three clusters defined by parents' work demands. We found no significant group differences for the high-father-demands group or for the low-demands group. As Figure 2.2

Figure 2.1. Mothers' and Fathers' Work Demands

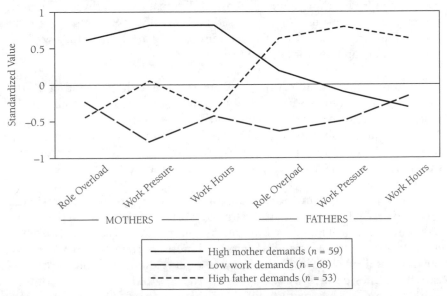

Source: Bumpus, Crouter, and McHale, 1999. Copyright 1999 by the National Council on Family Relations, 3989 Central Ave. NE, Suite 550, Minneapolis, MN 55421. Reprinted by permission.

shows, the action was in the high-maternal-demands families, where the tendency for older sisters to do more than their younger brothers and for younger sisters to do more than their older brothers was particularly pronounced. The fact that younger sisters in this cluster performed more housework than their older brothers is a particularly striking anomaly because, as can be seen in Figure 2.2, firstborns typically performed more housework than their younger siblings.

It is important to emphasize that the statistical interaction depicted in Figure 2.2 is a within-family effect. We ran separate 3 (work group) × 2 (firstborn gender) × 2 (second-born gender) ANOVAs for firstborns and second-borns to disentangle this interesting finding further. In these analyses, the significant three-way interaction emerged for second-borns' levels of involvement in housework, $F(2, 160) = 3.78$, $p < .05$. The interaction was not significant for firstborns, although it came close: $F(2, 160) = 1.91$, $p < .15$. Younger brothers with older sisters were uniformly low in terms of their involvement in housework across the three work groups. Younger sisters with older brothers stood out in the high-maternal-work-demands group by virtue of their high levels of involvement in household tasks. Tukey follow-up tests revealed that they performed significantly more housework than other second-borns in that group. This significant pattern did not emerge in the other two work groups, as was the case in the first analysis. Thus, the conclusion that stressed mothers lean on daughters for help, especially when a son is also present, is supported by the pattern of within-family differences in firstborn versus second-born siblings' involvement in housework and by between-family comparisons of younger girls' and boys' levels of involvement.

Figure 2.2. Differences Between Firstborns' and Second-Borns' Time Spent in Household Tasks as a Function of Sibling Sex Composition and Parents' Work Demands

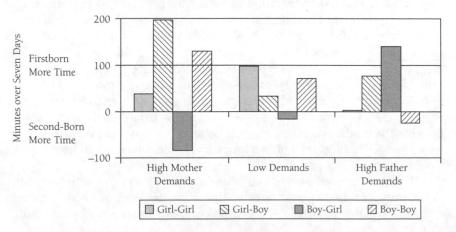

Is the Siblings' Division of Labor Related to Youths' Gender Role Attitudes? Having established that mothers' work demands may be one route through which a sex-typed division of labor develops between sisters and brothers, we were next interested in whether the siblings' division of labor was related to their attitudes about gender roles. Our working assumption was that parents' work circumstances give rise to children's household roles, which have implications for children's attitudes. It was important, however, to check first whether there were direct associations between parents' work circumstances and children's attitudes. A 3 (work group) × 2 (firstborn gender) × 2 (second-born gender) × 2 (sibling) mixed-model ANOVA, treating work group and the two siblings' genders as between-group factors, sibling as a within-group factor, and children's gender role attitudes as the dependent variable, revealed no associations between cluster membership and older or younger children's attitudes about gender roles.

It is conceivable, however, that parents' work helps to determine how much children get involved in housework and that children's attitudes in turn are influenced by the way in which they divide housework with their sibling. To explore this issue, we limited our analyses to the opposite-sex sibling pairs, reasoning that it is only in sibling pairs involving both a boy and a girl that siblings would have an opportunity to learn lessons about gender from the way in which housework is divided between them and their sibling. Imagine a second-born boy who performs much less household work than his older sibling. If that older sibling is a sister, the boy may acquire a view that housework is for women and girls and that sex-typed activity patterns in the family are normal and expected. If, on the other hand, that older sibling was a brother, the younger boy could not make gender-based attributions about sibling division of labor. Thus, we zeroed in on opposite-sex sibling pairs under the assumption that such dyads offered an opportunity for children both to experience more or less sex typing in the area of housework and to make gender-based attributions about it.

We first created a division-of-labor variable that reflected the proportion of tasks undertaken by either or both siblings that was performed by the girl, regardless of whether she was the older or the younger sibling. Higher values indicate that the division of labor was more traditional, that is, more dominated by the sister. In the forty-seven older sister–younger brother pairs, older sisters performed about 61 percent of the household tasks on average. The range was considerable, however: from 26 to 93 percent. In the forty-four older brother–younger sister pairs, second-born girls performed 49 percent of the tasks on average—virtually half of the tasks. But note that in these families, the girls were only about eight years old; they were younger siblings for whom a lower level of involvement in housework would be normative.

We first examined correlations between the traditionality of the division of labor and children's attitudes, separately for older sister–younger brother and older brother–younger sister pairs. When older sisters performed more housework relative to their younger brothers, those brothers' attitudes were more traditional ($r = .28$, $p < .06$), but there was no association between the division of labor and older sisters' attitudes. In addition, we found no significant associations for either sibling in older brother–younger sister families.

We were also interested in whether and how a traditional division of labor between two opposite-sex siblings was related to differences in the two siblings' attitudes about women's roles. Using median splits, we divided the sample into two groups: a traditional group in which girls performed the lion's share of the work and a nontraditional group in which the division was more equal. We then performed a 2 (sibling gender composition: older sister–younger brother versus older brother–younger sister) × 2 (sibling division of labor: traditional versus nontraditional) × 2 (sibling: firstborn versus second-born) mixed-model ANOVA, treating sibling as the repeated measure and siblings' gender role attitudes as the dependent variable. A significant three-way interaction indicated that differences between brothers' and sisters' attitudes about gender were more pronounced when there was a traditional division of labor ($F(1, 87) = 5.31$, $p < .02$; see Figure 2.3).

In interpreting Figure 2.3, it is important to keep in mind that as children develop, their gender role attitudes become less traditional, so there is a normative tendency in childhood and early adolescence for firstborns to be less traditional in outlook than their younger siblings (McHale, Updegraff, Helms-Erikson, and Crouter, 2001). In addition, in general, girls tend to hold less traditional attitudes about gender than boys do (McHale, Crouter, and Tucker, 1999). Figure 2.3 shows that in older sister–younger brother dyads, older sisters were consistently less traditional than their

Figure 2.3. Differences Between Firstborns' and Second-Borns' Gender Role Attitudes as a Function of Sibling Sex Composition and Siblings' Division of Labor

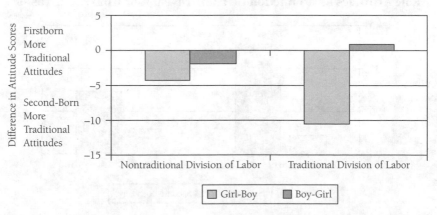

Note: Gender role attitudes were assessed using the Children's Attitudes Towards Women Scale. Scores can range from 19 to 76, with high scores reflecting more traditional attitudes.

younger brothers, as one would expect given the literature, but the gap between older sisters' and their younger brothers' attitudes was even more pronounced when their division of household labor was traditional than when it was nontraditional. In older brother–younger sister dyads, older brothers held less traditional attitudes than their younger sisters when the division of labor was nontraditional, but the two siblings were similar in attitudes when the division of labor was traditional. Figures 2.4 and 2.5 provide another perspective on these same data and indicate that boys' attitudes were related to the sibling division of labor, whereas girls' attitudes were not. As can be seen in Figure 2.4, older sisters' attitudes were similar regardless of whether the sibling division of labor was traditional or nontraditional, whereas their younger brothers' attitudes were more traditional when the division of labor was more traditional. Similarly, as can be seen in Figure 2.5, in older brother–younger sister pairs, younger sisters' attitudes were virtually the same in both conditions, but their older brothers held more traditional attitudes when the siblings maintained a traditional division of labor than when the division was more egalitarian.

Do Siblings' Gender Role Attitudes Predict the Sibling Division of Labor over Time, or Vice Versa? The concurrent findings, while intriguing, led us to confront the proverbial chicken-and-egg question: Does the way in which siblings divide housework shape brothers' and sisters' attitudes (and the difference between the two siblings' attitudes), or is the siblings' division of labor driven by children's attitudes? Third-variable explanations such as parents' work circumstances may play a role as well, although we think that they function primarily to set in motion certain family processes, such as the sibling division of labor, and that the division of

Figure 2.4. Firstborn Sisters' and Their Second-Born Brothers' Gender Role Attitudes as a Function of Their Division of Household Tasks

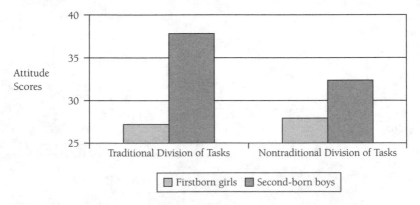

Note: Gender role attitudes were assessed using the Children's Attitudes Towards Women Scale. Scores can range from 19 to 76, with high scores reflecting more traditional attitudes.

labor may in turn influence children's attitudes. In a field study such as ours, it is not possible to identify causal relationships and directions of effect, even with longitudinal data; an experimental design with random assignment to conditions is needed in order to identify causal relationships definitively. Longitudinal analyses, however, are useful in building a case for one possible causal scenario or for eliminating another. With this in mind, we examined the associations between siblings' gender role attitudes and their division of labor over time, continuing to focus exclusively on the opposite-sex sibling pairs.

We first examined cross-time stability coefficients for our two central constructs. Not surprisingly, there was reasonably high stability in attitudes and even in the sibling division of labor from Year 1 to Year 3. The correlation over time was $r = .71$, $p < .001$, for firstborns' attitudes, and $r = .39$, $p < .001$, for second-borns' attitudes. The stability coefficient for the siblings' division of labor was $r = .41$, $p < .001$.

We next conducted a series of multiple regression analyses that focused on whether siblings' attitudes at Year 1 predicted the division of labor at Year 3 and whether the division of labor at Year 1 predicted the siblings' attitudes at Year 3. In these analyses, we consistently controlled for the Year 1 level of the criterion measure, one means of assessing relative change in that phenomenon. The first set of analyses predicted siblings' division of labor in Year 3. One analysis regressed the siblings' division of labor at Year 1, the sibling gender composition, the younger sibling's attitudes toward gender roles at Year 1, and the sibling gender composition × younger sibling's attitudes interaction term on the siblings' division of labor in Year 3. The second analysis in this set was exactly the

Figure 2.5. Firstborn Brothers' and Their Second-Born Sisters' Gender Role Attitudes as a Function of Their Division of Household Tasks

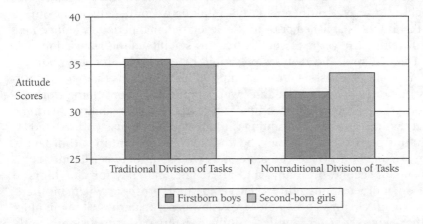

Note: Gender role attitudes were assessed using the Children's Attitudes Towards Women Scale. Scores can range from 19 to 76, with high scores reflecting more traditional attitudes.

same except that it focused on the older sibling's attitudes. The second set of analyses examined older and younger siblings' attitudes at Year 3 as the criterion measures. First, we predicted the younger sibling's attitudes at Year 3 by using the younger sibling's attitudes at Year 1, the sibling gender composition, the siblings' division of labor at Year 1, and the sibling gender composition × sibling division of labor interaction term as predictors. Second, a parallel analysis was performed substituting the older sibling's attitudes and gender as predictors.

The story that emerged from these cross-time regression analyses was consistent. These analyses revealed no significant cross-time associations between siblings' attitudes and their division of labor. In these models, siblings' attitudes at Year 1 did not predict the subsequent division of labor two years later, nor did the siblings' division of labor at Year 1 predict either sibling's subsequent gender role attitudes two years later. The interaction terms in all cases failed to reach statistical significance.

Recognizing that the main findings from the concurrent analyses pertained to the gap between brothers' and sisters' attitudes (a within-family phenomenon) rather than individual siblings' attitude levels, we took one more approach to our longitudinal data. We replicated the regression analyses described above, this time substituting the difference between the two siblings' attitudes (firstborn's score minus second-born's score) for the individual children's scores. Again, we were unable to predict relative change in either the siblings' division of labor or the gap in siblings' attitudes. The only significant predictors in these models were the Year 1 scores on the criterion measures in question (that is, cross-time stability) and the gender composition of the sibling dyad. Thus, we conclude that although there was a concurrent association between the siblings' division of labor and the difference between siblings' attitudes, as revealed by the analysis of variance results, there was no evidence that the division of labor predicted attitudes over time or that siblings' attitudes at Year 1 predicted the division of siblings' household tasks two years later. It is possible, however, that there is a causal link between these two phenomena but that it was established prior to the developmental period examined here and therefore that we are essentially tracking stability in this association.

Discussion. The analyses presented here provide mixed support for our original hypotheses. Our most important finding was that when mothers with both a son and a daughter were employed in demanding work situations, their daughters took on more household responsibilities, with the result that the gap between siblings' involvement in housework was greatest in this particular situation. The finding was apparent in within-family comparisons of brothers and sisters, as well as in between-family comparisons of second-born boys and girls. The tendency for daughters to take on more responsibility relative to their brothers when mothers' employment circumstances were stressful was particularly striking in older brother–younger sister families. Younger sisters performed significantly more housework than their older brothers in families where mothers reported high levels of work demands but not in other family types. The younger sisters in these families defied the age-related normative pattern for younger siblings to be less involved in housework than older siblings. Younger sisters in the high-maternal-work demands group also performed significantly more chores than other second-born youngsters when they had an older brother.

We do not know the family dynamics behind these gender-typed activity patterns. Do mothers who are busy and stressed actively turn to their daughters for help? Do daughters actively step in and volunteer their assistance? Do sons in these families actively resist involvement in housework or passively offer so little cooperation that busy mothers give up trying to engage them in high levels of housework participation? These scenarios are not mutually exclusive; indeed, they may all operate together to create the observed patterns. It will be important in future generations of research on children's time use to move beyond counting the number of minutes children engage in various activities to ask other questions, such as who initiated the activity in question (for example, did the child volunteer to set the table, or did the mother ask him to do it?) and how much the actor enjoyed participating in the activity (for example, did the child find satisfaction in mowing the lawn or resent having to do it?). Research on husbands' and wives' participation in household tasks indicates that sometimes women equate performing these activities with providing care and support to family members (DeVault, 1991). We need to learn more about how daughters— and sons—interpret their involvement in these activities.

We also found cross-sectional evidence that the siblings' division of labor and their attitudes about gender roles are linked. In these analyses, we focused just on the older brother–younger sister and older sister–younger brother sibling pairs, reasoning that it takes having both a boy and girl present in the family for the siblings' division of labor to present lessons about gender. Using mixed-model analysis of variance that enabled us to make within-family as well as between-family comparisons, we found that the gap in siblings' attitudes was significantly greater in families in which girls were shouldering a greater share of the division of household tasks. The attitude gap in this case reflected the tendency for boys to hold relatively more traditional attitudes. Sisters' attitudes, in contrast, were similar in both division-of-labor situations. Thus, we found evidence for an association between siblings' division of labor and at least boys' attitudes about gender with cross-sectional data from Year 1.

It is tempting to attribute a causal relationship to associations of this kind. To double-check this finding, we examined associations over time. We asked whether, controlling for the division of labor in Year 1, attitudes in Year 1 predicted the division of labor in Year 3; we also examined whether, controlling for attitudes in Year 1, the division of labor predicted attitudes in Year 3. We used a similar approach to examine the difference between older and younger siblings' attitudes. No matter how we examined the cross-time associations, the conclusion was always the same. We found stability over time in youngsters' attitudes and stability over time in how siblings divided household chores, but attitudes in Year 1 did not predict how siblings divided chores two years later beyond stability, and the division of labor in Year 1 did not predict siblings' attitudes two years later.

Why were we unsuccessful in demonstrating associations between attitudes and the division of housework over time? There is a host of possible reasons, some conceptual and some methodological. On a conceptual level, it is possible that we came on the developmental scene too late to capture the causal process. Children's attitudes may have been shaped (in part) by prior involvement in household tasks by the two siblings. The high level of stability over time in children's attitudes, especially for the firstborns, suggests that at least by age eleven, these attitudes may not be highly malleable. If this is the case, it is perhaps not surprising that we were unable to predict attitudes with prior data on the sibling division of labor or to predict the sibling division of labor with prior data on attitudes.

It is also possible, of course, that other phenomena are more important sources of influence on adolescents' attitudes about gender roles besides the way in which siblings divide housework. Throughout childhood and adolescence, youngsters encounter messages about gender roles not only within the family but at school, in their peer groups, in their leisure activities, and through the media (Huston, 1983; Ruble and Martin, 1998). Even within the family, there are numerous other, potentially more powerful sources of gender socialization besides the sibling division of household tasks, including how mothers and fathers divide paid and unpaid work between themselves, the kinds of free-time activities that mothers and fathers engage in with and without their children, how mothers and fathers allocate their time between their sons and their daughters, and mothers' and fathers' own attitudes about gender roles. Thus, on its own, the sibling division of labor may not be a potent enough socialization experience to be linked to children's developing attitudes in the long run.

It is also possible that different children react to the siblings' division of labor in different ways. For example, some girls who find themselves doing it all may accept the status quo and develop more traditional attitudes about gender roles over time. Others, however, may resent their greater involvement in housework relative to their brothers', and their attitudes may thus become less traditional over time, reflecting this consciousness-raising process. To the extent that these two groups of girls react differently to the same objective phenomenon (that is, the siblings' division of labor), they may cancel each other out, resulting in a null finding. Thus, it would be important in future research to learn more about children's attributions with regard to the way housework is divided in their family.

There are other methodological considerations as well. By focusing only on opposite-sex dyads, we reduced our sample by half and lost statistical power, making it more difficult to detect significant associations. We think it is important to zero in on opposite-sex siblings when asking questions about gender socialization, but future studies should recruit larger numbers of same- and opposite-sex sibling pairs. It is also worth noting that in about a third of the families, there were more than two siblings present. We focused on the division of labor between the two eldest siblings, which makes sense given their age and maturity. But the possible roles of third, fourth, and fifth siblings (and so on) may be important to consider when mapping out the division of labor among siblings. Perhaps for some second-born siblings, the relevant comparison is between them and a younger sibling, not between them and the firstborn sibling. We currently do not gather data on the daily activities of other siblings in the family beyond the first-born and second-born. Collecting such data would present logistical and analytical challenges, but such information would more accurately and completely assess how children's housework is organized in the family.

Conclusion

The data presented here make a case for the importance of building within-family comparisons into research on family socialization patterns. The ability to compare and contrast the level of involvement in housework of two siblings in each family revealed that in middle childhood, sisters and brothers experience the most gender-typed division of labor within the family when their mothers are in demanding work circumstances. We need to learn more about the family processes that underlie this pattern. We also found that in opposite-sex sibling pairs, the sibling division of labor is linked to children's attitudes about gender roles, at least concurrently. This association, however, did not hold up over time when we examined youngsters' attitudes and involvement in housework two years later. Understanding the familial and extrafamilial conditions that give rise to the development of children's and adolescents' gender role attitudes as they unfold over time is high on the agenda for our future research.

References

Antill, J., Cotton, S., Goodnow, J., and Russell, G. "Measures of Children's Sex-Typing in Middle Childhood II." Unpublished manuscript, Macquarie University, Sydney, Australia, 1994.

Bumpus, M. F., Crouter, A. C., and McHale, S. M. "Work Demands of Dual-Earner Couples: Implications for Parents' Knowledge About Children's Daily Lives in Middle Childhood." *Journal of Marriage and the Family*, 1999, *61*(2), 465–475.

Coltrane, S. "Research on Household Labor: Modeling and Measuring the Social Embeddedness of Routine Family Work." *Journal of Marriage and the Family*, 2000, *62*, 1208–1233.

Crouter, A. C., Maguire, M. C., Helms-Erikson, H., and McHale, S. M. "Parental Work in Middle Childhood: Links Between Employment and the Division of Housework, Parent-Child Activities and Parental Monitoring." In T. B. Parcel (ed.), *Research in the Sociology of Work*, Vol. 7: *Work and Family*. Greenwich, Conn.: JAI Press, 1999.

Crouter, A. C., Manke, B. A., and McHale, S. M. "The Family Context of Gender Intensification in Early Adolescence." *Child Development*, 1995, *66*, 317–329.

DeVault, M. *Feeding the Family: The Social Organization of Caring as Gendered Work.* Chicago: University of Chicago Press, 1991.

Ferree, M. M. "Beyond Separate Spheres: Feminism and Family Research." *Journal of Marriage and the Family*, 1990, *52*, 866–884.

Goode, W. J. "Why Men Resist." In B. Thorne (ed.), *Rethinking the Family: Some Feminist Questions.* White Plains, N.Y.: Longman, 1982.

Goodnow, J. "Children's Household Work: Its Nature and Functions." *Psychological Bulletin*, 1988, *103*, 5–26.

Huston, A. C. "Sex-Typing." In P. Mussen (series ed.) and E. M. Hetherington (vol. ed.), *Handbook of Child Psychology*, Vol. 4: *Socialization, Personality, and Social Development.* (4th ed.) New York: Wiley, 1983.

Larson, R. W., and Verma, S. "How Children and Adolescents Spend Time Across the World: Work, Play, and Developmental Opportunities." *Psychological Bulletin*, 1999, *125*, 701–736.

Manke, B., Seery, B. L., Crouter, A. C., and McHale, S. M. "The Three Corners of Domestic Labor: Mothers', Fathers', and Children's Weekday and Weekend Housework." *Journal of Marriage and the Family*, 1994, *56*, 657–668.

McHale, S. M., Crouter, A. C., and Bartko, W. T. "Traditional and Egalitarian Patterns of Parental Involvement: Antecedents, Consequences, and Temporal Rhythms." In D. Featherman, R. Lerner, and M. Perlmutter (eds.), *Life-Span Development and Behavior.* Vol. 11. Hillsdale, N.J.: Erlbaum, 1992.

McHale, S. M., Crouter, A. C., and Tucker, C. J. "Family Context and Gender Role Socialization in Middle Childhood: Comparing Girls to Boys and Sisters to Brothers." *Child Development*, 1999, *70*, 990–1004.

McHale, S. M., Updegraff, K. A., Helms-Erikson, H., and Crouter, A. C. "Sibling Influences on Gender Development in Middle Childhood and Early Adolescence: A Longitudinal Study." *Developmental Psychology*, 2001, *37*, 115–125.

Medrich, E. A., Roizen, J., Rubin, V., and Buckley, S. *The Serious Business of Growing Up.* Berkeley: University of California Press, 1982.

Moos, R. H. *Work Environment Scale Manual.* (2nd ed.) Palo Alto, Calif.: Consulting Psychologists Press, 1986.

Parcel, T. B., and Menaghan, E. G. *Parents' Jobs and Children's Lives.* Hawthorne, N.Y.: Aldine de Gruyter, 1994.

Perry-Jenkins, M., Repetti, R. L., and Crouter, A. C. "Work and Family in the 1990s." *Journal of Marriage and the Family*, 2000, *62*, 981–998.

Reilly, M. D. "Working Wives and Convenience Consumption." *Journal of Consumer Research*, 1982, *8*, 407–418.

Ruble, D. N., and Martin, C. M. "Gender Development." In W. Damon (series ed.) and N. Eisenberg (vol. ed.), *The Handbook of Child Psychology*, Vol. 3: *Social, Emotional, and Personality Development.* (5th ed.) New York: Wiley, 1998.

Starrels, M. E. "Gender Differences in Parent-Child Relations." *Journal of Family Issues*, 1994, *15*, 148–165.

West, C., and Zimmerman, D. "Doing Gender." *Gender and Society*, 1987, *1*, 125–151.

White, L. K., and Brinkerhoff, D. B. "The Sexual Division of Labor: Evidence from Childhood." *Social Forces*, 1981, *60*, 170–181.

Whiting, B., and Whiting, J. *Children of Six Cultures: A Psycho-Cultural Analysis.* Cambridge, Mass.: Harvard University Press, 1975.

ANN C. CROUTER is professor of human development at the Pennsylvania State University and codirector of the Penn State Family Relationships Project.

MELISSA R. HEAD is a doctoral candidate in human development and family studies at the Pennsylvania State University.

MATTHEW F. BUMPUS is assistant professor of human development at California State University at Chico.

SUSAN M. MCHALE is professor of human development at the Pennsylvania State University and codirector of the Penn State Family Relationships Project.

3

Young people's ideas about their obligations to parents are linked to the popularization of high school as an institutional space for adolescence. This chapter examines the growing acceptance of the concept of adolescence among Italian immigrants historically as a salient example of a broader cultural change.

Extended Schooling, Adolescence, and the Renegotiation of Responsibility Among Italian Immigrant Families in New Haven, Connecticut, 1910–1940

Stephen Lassonde

One of the quiet cultural transformations of the twentieth century in the United States has been the acceptance in all groups of the meaningfulness of age gradations among children and youths (Kett, 1977; Chudacoff, 1989; Mirel, 1991). Who could have predicted at the dawn of the twentieth century the swift success of the "adolescent idea" and the subdivision of stages in growing up that has occurred since (Cole and Cole, 1996)? Schooling, the most pervasive of all modern institutions, has had the greatest influence on the willingness of Americans to think through novel categories of cognitive, emotional, and physiological growth and well-being in young people. While the passage and enforcement of compulsory schooling and a concomitant need to make distinctions among children's school performance (which soon led to age grading) established the framework for thinking about pupils developmentally, it was the voluntary extension of schooling that proved the true measure of parents' willing adoption of the developmental view. The critical period of growth in schooling beyond the minimum required by law occurred between 1910 and 1940, when high school attendance grew dramatically.

How did working-class youths, who formed the largest pool of potential high school recruits, experience this change in their own families, where schooling often conflicted with parents' ideas about the usefulness of education, as well as with a conception of children's maturation that insisted on early accountability to family material need? Within the U.S. working class of the early twentieth century, differences in attitudes toward schooling have been most readily expressed as owing to the predispositions of ethnic and racial groups. Little studied, however, is the influence of rising levels of high school attendance on age norms within and across ethnic groups, a trend that gathered increasing force with each passing decade (Thernstrom, 1964; Smith, 1969; Olneck and Lazerson, 1974; Hogan, 1978; Perlmann, 1988; Cohen, 1992).

While a survey across and within ethnic groups in the United States during this period would provide the most complete picture of the variety and pace of changing attitudes toward the popular adoption of the developmental paradigm and the connection of the concept of adolescence to high school attendance, the richest historical data are recoverable only through painstaking work in interview materials. Assembling such a picture is made more difficult by the fact that the documentary record is spotty and uneven in quality. In the recent past, historians have chosen to infer attitudes from behavior to make comparisons across subgroups, but it is useful nonetheless to employ what limited historical records exist to gain a more nuanced understanding of the depth and complexity of attitudinal change and its relationship to behavior (Perlmann, 1988).

Southern Italian immigrants (*contadini,* as they were known, because the vast majority of them emigrated from the Italian countryside) provide an excellent case study for exploring the connection between persistence in high school and changing age norms. It has been shown repeatedly that southern Italian immigrants were the least enthusiastic of all ethnic groups about sending their children to school, and their children attained the lowest average grade levels among the subgroups in the United States during the first half of the twentieth century. Consequently, Italians and their children were the favorite subject of educators and sociologists during this period, so the documentary record for this group is relatively ample (Olneck and Lazerson, 1974; Hogan, 1978; Perlmann, 1988; Cohen, 1992). Moreover, the *contadini* clearly articulated their reasons for rejecting school, so it is possible from first-person accounts and interviews to reconstruct their attitudes about education in ways that are not possible for other groups (Lassonde, 1994).

Historians have shown decisively the long-term economic significance of early school leaving for immigrant children: intergenerational upward social mobility was slower for Italian immigrants than for any other white subgroup in the United States during the first third of the twentieth century (Perlmann, 1988; Barton, 1975). The children of southern Italian immigrants in New Haven, Connecticut, were no exception. They quit school at an earlier age than any other group, performed on average more poorly than any other group in the city's schools, had the highest levels of truancy and delinquency, and entered the workforce at the earliest age. Among their parents, illiteracy was common, and their parents' exposure to schooling was more limited than any other immigrant group (New Haven Board of Education, 1908–1932; Cutts, 1933). The southern Italian family economy, which exhibited all the traits of what might best be characterized as traditional agrarian attitudes toward familial reciprocity—stressing age and gender hierarchy, the expectation of children's contributions to family subsistence from an early age, and a steady rather than step-wise emergence into the obligations of adult life—collided in this period with the emerging developmental perspective and its more forgiving scheme of children's obligations to parents and other kin.

Still, the rising tendency to prolong children's education happened within a specific political economy; it did not occur because it had been mandated from above but because it became necessary, possible, and, finally, even desirable in the eyes of some immigrant parents (Altenbaugh, 1993; Perlmann, 1988). Indeed, as historian David Levine has shrewdly observed of the slow and unsteady rise of the ideal of the "sentimentalized" child among working-class parents, their reluctance to continue their children in school was not the result of an unwillingness to invest in them emotionally or materially. Rather (and this was doubly true of working-class Italian immigrants in the United States), they could not afford to place demonstrative symbols of affection for their children (like extended schooling) above household subsistence or to threaten time-honored lessons on the virtue of collective strivings (Levine, 1987). Italian immigrant parents in the United States could not afford—materially or "morally"—to extend their sons' and daughters' schooling or the accompanying developmental perspective that newly furnished an ethical basis for doing so. This chapter provides a snapshot of two periods, before and after World War I: pictures of the way southern Italian immigrant parents and their children thought about schooling during a period of dynamic change, when a high school education was becoming but had not yet attained its status as a minimal credential for most occupations.

The *Contadini* in New Haven

Despite meaningful gains in grade attainment during the first three decades of the twentieth century, Italian immigrants in New Haven began the century profoundly skeptical about what education had to offer their children, and for many, this wariness persisted. Partly this owed to their own inexperience with schooling and partly to its irrelevance to the economy of their existence in their home villages in Abruzzi, Apulia, Basilicata, Calabria, and Campania. Rates of illiteracy in these regions ranged from 70 percent to 90 percent during the period of heaviest emigration. Although schooling in

Italy had been made compulsory by 1877, the law was virtually unenforced until the 1920s in the south, and as a consequence, elementary schooling existed solely for the benefit of the children of the *galantuomo* class—craftsmen, merchants, landlords, and government officials. The children of the *contadini* were supposed to work in the fields and help their parents at home. Therefore, even the most highly educated among them were considered well schooled if they were able to read, write, add, and subtract. More schooling than this was deemed neither necessary nor desirable (Covello, 1967; Banfield, 1958).

As a consequence of prejudice, unfamiliarity, and a strictly utilitarian view of education, southern Italian immigrant parents believed that the consignment of their children to school threatened not only to create economic hardship but taught their children the wrong lessons about their obligations to others. In this respect, *contadini* parents at the turn of the century differed little from their working-class predecessors in the United States, many of whom had resisted the introduction and enforcement of compulsory schooling from the 1870s to the end of the century (Lassonde, 1996). However, whereas compulsory school attendance and the legal apparatus that supported it were phased in gradually over the latter half of the nineteenth century in Connecticut, immigrant families arriving after 1900 encountered a highly integrated system of enforcement. It was a system that mobilized and coordinated the efforts of state and city educators, civic officials, employers, local police, truant officers, and the judiciary to commit children to school until age fourteen.

New Haven's newest immigrants, moreover, entered a city alive to the potential threat posed by the introduction of non-English-speaking children into the district. Although children of Italian immigrants occupied no more than a handful of the city's schools during the early 1890s, when Italians numbered just over two thousand (but after a decade in which the city's school-age population had increased by one-third), the superintendent of schools complained noisily about the ignorance and illiteracy of foreign-born parents and their disregard of school laws. New Haven's population, he said, which was "increasing and promiscuous . . . containing a large foreign element," had recently witnessed an "influx . . . [of] . . . people who were ignorant of our institutions, laws, language, people who had not been accustomed to send their children to school in the country from whence they came and who seemed to care but little for their education, especially in the English language" (New Haven Board of Education, 1898, p. 24). In 1908, when Italian immigrants and their children had increased to almost twenty-two thousand, the New Haven Board of Education conducted its first full census of pupil nationality, and in 1915 it initiated an annual survey of the public schools' ethnic composition. By 1920, Italian immigrants were the most populous ethnic group in the city, at 34,558. Yet even these figures do not adequately convey the dramatic influx of Italian immigrant children into the public school system, since nearly one-half of all pupils enrolled in the city schools that year were of Italian descent (Racca, "Ethnography," n.d.; Myers, 1950).

As their numbers swelled, *contadini* parents developed a reputation among school visitors for being indifferent to their children's performance in school and, worse, fixated on their pecuniary worth. As late as the 1930s, when Italian immigrant children's persistence in school began to rival that of other groups, they still labored under impressions formed by city school officials at the turn of the century as being uninterested and undistinguished in academic subjects (Whitelaw, 1935). Given this rapidly changing climate of social norms in the Italian immigrant community, how was schooling understood by Italian immigrant parents as secondary education increasingly became the average experience? How did these parents respond to the constraints imposed on the economic and emotional organization of their family lives? How did the changing educational aspirations of their children reconfigure this matrix? And finally, what did these parents make of the state's imposition of the developmental paradigm?

Conceptions of Age in the *Contadini* Family Economy

The "idleness" conferred on children who attended school in America—especially as they approached the age at which they could legally contribute to family income—was a challenge to the *contadino*'s most basic understanding of human relations. Heretofore unquestioned elements of power and sentiment in family life were thrust on them: the respect of children for the authority of parents, the prerogatives of age, male privilege, and, most generally, a sense of devotion to parental welfare as the center of a child's concerns. Thus, expressions of astonishment at the reversal of the order of things—so characteristic of southern Italian immigrant parents' reactions to the length of schooling in the United States—encapsulated two basic reactions, according to Covello (1967): the disturbing priority given to children in American society (and its implicit dangers) and alarm at the role of the state in imposing and maintaining what Italian parents regarded as an insidious dependence of children on their parents. In addition to upsetting a sociocultural tradition in the provinces of southern Italy that viewed education in the most narrowly pragmatic terms, schooling in America implied a conception of children's roles that clashed with Italian immigrants' ideas about age and familial responsibility. The variety of distinctions between age groups in the United States and the role of the schools in extending and upholding these threatened deeply held convictions about the process of socializing young people.

Covello's (1967) penetrating appraisal of adolescence as seen through the eyes of southern Italian immigrants displays a remarkable acuity about the constructedness of childhood, adolescence, and youth in the United States. Indeed, in a way that surpasses contemporaneous reflections on the rising significance of adolescence, Covello's vivid portrait of the southern

Italian parent's perplexity at children's "idleness" in the United States renders the exoticism of psychologized cultural constructions of human growth in a manner that rivals Margaret Mead's examination of youthful rites of passage in far-off Samoa (Mead, 1928). "The status of American youth," observed Covello (1967), "amazed" the *contadino*, "but also filled him with apprehension. . . . Boys and even girls, were compelled to go to school up to a certain age regardless of parental feelings, the child's aptitudes and desires. Below a certain age, work by children was prohibited. And when the child neither goes to school nor attends to useful work, the enforced leisure and idleness detach the child from the orbit of family life and remove him from the wholesome influence of familial tradition" (p. 289).

More familiar to southern Italian immigrant families was a process of incremental, seamless emergence into adult society, "as gradual and uneventful as . . . [the] physical transformation of the infant into an adult. . . . There were no sharp age divisions, each shaded with the older and the younger." There were fundamentally "two groups," Covello says, "children and adults: helpless infants and very old feeble folks (and playful tots, young men and young women) but never what we call [adolescents]" (Covello, n.d., folder 17). Where the father was sufficiently comfortable financially and the sole earner in the family, "the parent could indulge a sentimental attitude toward the adolescent and make a concession to the social pattern of America. But most were not in this position." Of greater significance, in any case, he concludes,

> The American school system . . . created a group of idle [youths]. . . . The old Italian equilibrium in which adolescents [fit] well and in a useful way into the family struct[ure] and its economy, had entirely broken; youth was hardly [any] longer an integral part of the Italian family institution. From the ages of seven to fourteen years of age, it was said, the Italian boy in American society did nothing but play in the streets. [Covello, 1967, p. 289]

This perception expressed the general frustration of many Italian immigrant parents who felt that the indiscriminate compulsion of schooling, apart from depriving families of needed income, failed to recognize the variability of children's inclination toward formal learning and forced the same lengthy course of schooling on all (Covello, 1967).

Play among *contadini* children had always been directed toward some useful activity, such as participating in the harvesting of grapes or making a game out of clearing stones from a field (Covello, 1967). By the same token, the extent to which boys played in the streets in America—and the fact that they had so much spare time—grated against the familiar rhythms of children's diurnal obligations in southern Italy. "I don't remember [that] we ever played ball, or cops and robbers, or hide-and-seek games," a Sicilian immigrant told Covello. "We were supposed to play only such games as would be of use when we grew up"(Covello,

1967, p. 269). At an early age, between six and eight years old, children were supposed to be occupied with chores and activities that would establish a lifelong sense of responsibility. This "responsible work" meant that "the child (even considering his age) was also a real worker who used real tools, like those of adults except for their size" (Covello, 1967, p. 265). The variety of skills that had been required to maintain the status of a peasant, fisherman, or even a craftsman in southern Italy could be learned at an early age in the parental household or by apprenticeship. Therefore, Covello (1967) points out, formal education was regarded as superfluous, since such skills and techniques as there were in a peasant economy required only the most straightforward transmission from father to son or from mother to daughter. And finally, the role of schooling in laying a foundation for a "moral" upbringing—one of the fundamental purposes of all rudimentary systems of mass schooling—was viewed as redundant at best but potentially insidious as well. The moral code in a relatively homogeneous society, he says, was a "reasonably uniform body of rules learned in daily contact and social relations. The moral customs, unshaken for centuries, were effectively transmitted, without any stimulation of a person's logical faculties. . . . Beyond a few proverbs, some legends and other bits of generalized wisdom, [formalized] knowledge was at some distance from popular comprehension and consumption (Covello, n.d., folder 17).

As a rule, the upper limit of schooling for immigrants from the south was about three or four years—and even less for the *contadini*. Beyond this, a couple of children in a family might receive training in a trade, which, for boys, often depended on the specific skills possessed by older family members. With girls, dressmaking was invariably prized as both a marketable skill and a money saver in cash-poor households. Although the females of all poor households did the finishing work on their family's clothing, the more sophisticated tasks such as pattern making and cutting were, even in the poorest households, performed by a dressmaker or tailor. In essence, boys and girls of the *contadini* underwent a kind of apprenticeship from age seven or eight forward. Boys were given a small herd of sheep to tend and helped with the harvest, and girls followed their mothers around the house doing small chores all day long.

The children of artisans, on the other hand, ordinarily attended school for a few years because they lived in the towns and could conveniently do so, but concurrently they would work in the shop of a blacksmith, barber, or shoemaker. They cleaned and performed other trivial chores in these shops for virtually no pay. Most often, this sort of arrangement was made with a relative, which reinforced the familial aspect of training, discipline, and respect for authority in the eyes of the child. The trade skills acquired could be specifically useful as the child matured, but the most important element of this regime, according to Covello (1967), was the lesson "that he who does not work does not eat" (p. 270).

The Relationship of Schooling to Other Institutions in Italy and the United States

The differences between the kinds of education imparted in southern Italy and in the United States were especially palpable to adult immigrants who had had little schooling in southern Italy. There had been a pronounced continuity in Italy between the moral didacticism promoted by the schools and the emphasis on respect for parental (and particularly paternal) wishes at home. Schooling in both countries was described by immigrants as "severe," but in different ways. The American schools were unyielding in their insistence on enrollment and attendance, not realizing that children's absences often meant the difference between family subsistence and privation; the Italian schools, by contrast, were uncompromising in their attention to discipline and outward displays of deference to authority, a concern in the estimation of immigrant parents that was in perilously short supply in the American schools (Covello, n.d., folder 16; Williams, 1938). Thus, Italian immigrant parents commonly voiced disenchantment with American schools for failing to reinforce the code of discipline they maintained at home. In their own villages, they could have counted on the adults of the community to uphold the values of respect for elders, one's parents, and family honor (Bell, 1979). The village church reinforced the same code. But in the United States, southern Italians were often at odds with the Catholic church and thought that the public schools were too permissive (Vecoli, 1969; Orsi, 1985).

American schools did a good job of teaching their children, it was widely admitted, but a typical lament was expressed by a man who reflected, "What good is it if a boy is bright and intelligent, and then does not know enough to respect his family. Such a boy would be worth nothing! That's the trouble with American kids; they're smart, but the schools don't teach them to respect their families" (Covello, n.d., folder 18). Worry about a relative lack of discipline in the schools translated into a further sense that American schools were insufficiently serious. Again, although many parents were satisfied with the academic emphasis of the American schools, others felt that whatever scholarly discipline might be instilled in their children was simultaneously undercut by a distracting focus on frivolous nonpedagogical activities. One mother complained that "when you pass by a school all you hear is singing or the steps of dancing, or the noise of playing, playing, playing" (Racca, "Ethnography," n.d., p. 32). Another instance of the seeming frivolousness of American schools (in the opinion of this same mother) was the way her daughter's teacher one year had instructed every girl in the classroom to bring a present for a boy classmate at Christmas. This request seemed to her to epitomize the shortcomings of schooling in America and provoked the woman to remark: "As if there were not [already] enough love-making in the American schools!" (Racca, "Ethnography," n.d., p. 32). Thus, the significant contributions made by children to household and agricultural tasks in Italy—herding sheep, weeding, harvesting, and stone clearing for peasant boys; making and repairing lines and nets in fisherman families; and for all girls, cleaning, cooking, sewing, spinning, mending, and finishing garments—served as fundamental training for children. Taken together, these tasks were closer to the sense of education held by southern Italian immigrants than was the formal, routinized education offered by schooling in the United States (Williams, 1938; Covello, 1967).

Birth Order and Gender

Historians have identified a tendency among immigrant families in the United States since the middle of the nineteenth century to extend the schooling of younger children at the expense of older siblings. One explanation for this pattern is that younger children simply benefited from the relatively higher income of households that had reached the later phases of the family cycle. As older children entered the workforce, the household reached its peak earning capacity and could afford to keep the younger ones in school. In addition, it has been suggested that this trend reflected gradual acculturation. Historians have shown that immigrant groups arriving during the middle of the nineteenth century—preeminently the Irish—wished, as soon as they could, to consume like Yankee working-class families. Initially, they accomplished this by sending their children out to work, but later, when male household heads earned a larger income, they reversed the pattern and lengthened schooling to the extent feasible for all children. Birth order rather than gender seems to have been the key determinant within these families in choosing among children to be schooled (Modell, 1978; Bodnar, 1980; Clubb, Austin, and Kirk, 1989; Glenn, 1990).

Although birth order was undoubtedly a significant dimension of family educational strategies among southern Italians in the United States, there seems to have been a stronger gender bias at work as well: a greater reluctance to school girls than was the case in most other ethnic groups. According to Covello, this arose from the conviction that educating girls was "economically disastrous" (Covello, 1967, p. 292). While supporting a boy of twelve in school (and thus forgoing his contribution to the household economy) seemed wrong in the eyes of Italian immigrant parents, it was inconceivable that girls should receive anything beyond the most rudimentary education (Covello, n.d., folder 17). Therefore, keeping a girl in school until the age of fourteen, Covello (1967) observed, was "a source of constant irritation and anger to her parents." Because boys traditionally enjoyed privileges never extended to girls, explained one mother, "the idea of [boys] . . . going to school instead of helping us [parents] was only half bad. Boys somehow managed to make a penny or two. . . . But when girls at thirteen and fourteen wasted good time in school, it simply made us regret our coming to America" (Covello, 1967, p. 292).

Immigrant *contadini* parents, when they thought they could get away with it, discouraged girls from attending school at all. Covello cites an instance in which a ten-year-old girl was forbidden by her father from going to school because he needed her help in running his restaurant. In the father's estimation, "She could read and write, and that was enough for any Italian girl." The father insisted that "she was big enough to give real help to her parents" (Covello, 1967, p. 293). By removing a girl from her "customary functions of the home," schooling upset the structure of the family economy. Thus, the bitter opposition of southern Italian immigrants to girls' schooling may have stemmed additionally from the consequent necessity of forcing the mother to work outside the home. This situation, as Yans-McLaughlin (1977) has emphasized, was viewed as a cause for shame in Italian immigrant families.

Another source of moral difficulty presented by schooling girls was the perceived danger of rendering a girl unmarriageable by placing her in situations where she might be vulnerable to male improprieties. In southern Italy, not only was coeducation unthinkable for this reason, it was also feared that simply teaching a girl how to write would afford access to males beyond the family's surveillance. Girls' literacy was thought to incite amorous correspondence between girls and boys and therefore had the potential to bring shame on the family, imperiling not only a girl's own reputation and marriageability but that of her sisters as well (Covello, 1967; Yans-McLaughlin, 1977). Southern Italian families considered it highly improper for a girl even to be seen on the street with any nonfamily male. Older girls and boys were not to speak or communicate in any way with one another. A girl's family was supposed to mediate any interaction she might have with the opposite sex. Above all, it was believed that a girl and a boy must never be left alone together because the sexual impulse was considered so potent that it might easily overpower them (Covello, 1967; J. Palmieri, interview with the author, May 16, 1990).

In the northeastern United States, where education was compulsory to age fourteen and the voluntary extension of schooling beyond the legal minimum was approaching the status of a social norm for most adolescents by the mid-1920s, the daughters of Italian immigrants often had to fight to remain in school. Indeed, a girl who stayed in school against the wishes of her parents normally did so at the cost of the relative autonomy she possessed as a household wage earner. An extreme but instructive example of this principle is illustrated by the story of Beppa Giacomini. Beppa left Italy at the age of fourteen to join her father and brothers in New Haven during the 1910s. Knowing how enthusiastic she had been about school as a child in Italy, her brothers urged her to enroll in public school in New Haven on her arrival. Yet unbeknown to her, well before she had left Italy, her father, a compulsive drinker, had offered her in marriage to whichever of his drinking companions would buy him the most drinks. Eventually, one of these men (someone from her village who had known Beppa since childhood) bought her father so many drinks that he was compelled to promise her in marriage to this man. Once informed of the arrangement, however, Beppa realized that if she had "stayed home [and attended school] she would have been dependent upon her family and obliged to do as they pleased." By going to work, she saw that "she would be independent and if there was to be a fight [about her father's promise] she would be able to support herself. So it was that three days after she arrived in America she went to work" (Racca, "Selected Family Histories," n.d., p. 29).

Yet even in more mundane circumstances, daughters' educational aspirations were dismissed out of hand. Extended schooling for girls clearly represented an intolerable degree of autonomy—a radical departure from expectations commonly held by Italian parents for their daughters and so removed from their conception of the purpose of schooling. A girl who proposed to pursue schooling beyond the minimum required by law necessarily sacrificed the financial and emotional support that she might have counted on had she chosen the more traditional path. On the other hand, the case of Beppa demonstrates the advantage of choosing work as a way of purchasing some semblance of liberation from a father's abusive exercise of authority. Wage earning, in contrast to schooling, offered immediate leverage. First, it fulfilled parental expectations and extended to parents some reparation for having nurtured children during their years of dependence. Second, it offered a tangible basis for renegotiating the implicit contract of reciprocity between parents and children, however unequal the terms.

Finally, broader differences in parental attitudes toward the schooling of girls and boys stemmed—at least formally—from a very basic material consideration. Boys, once married, still "belonged" to the family and could help their parents if necessary. Girls, on the other hand, were considered "lost" to their husband's family once they married (Smith, 1985; Child, 1939; Williams, 1938). Any material assistance to parents or displays of loyalty were properly directed to a married daughter's husband's family. This factor put added pressure on parents to obtain what material assistance they could from their daughters before they married and therefore discouraged them from supporting girls' education, not to mention professional ambitions. Consequently, girls who harbored aspirations that included schooling beyond the age of compulsory attendance were considered ridiculous. It was impractical from the parents' point of view because it deprived them of income, and it was pointless as well because, as one young woman's parents put it, "What's the use of educating them, they will get married and then who will know whether they are educated or not?" (Covello, n.d., folder 16, p. 11). Moreover, it was feared that educated girls would become too selfish—an attitude that would later hamper their maternal aptitudes. "What *happens* when you send a girl to high school, or even to college?" asked one woman.

She earns money and does not give money to her mother. That's breaking down the *mortalità* of the family. Shouldn't the family get some profit from

all the *sforzi* [effort] that her family has made? This is a bad American custom. The children owe something to their parents. It was a case of the mother,
"give, give, give," and the girl "take, take, take" and no return. How can children be brought up right in this way? And [how] . . . are the girls going to
bring up their children? Things will go from bad to worse. *"Ognuna per i Conti
Suoi"* ["each one for his own affairs"]. Ther[e] is no family, nor anything!
[Covello, n.d., folder 17]

"The Italians have the idea that one or two of their sons might become
big businessmen while the others should go to work early," remarked a New
Haven–born son of Italian immigrants in his twenties during the late 1930s,
when he was interviewed by social psychologist Irvin L. Child (1939). Child
inquired, "Which one [of his sons] is supposed to go into business?" The
reply was, "Whoever has the most brains." Child then asked, "Do they have
that idea in your family?" The reply was, "Yes . . . but we got in a hole and
couldn't do anything about it" (Child, 1939, p. 462). Covello contended that
even for Italian immigrant sons, educational prerogatives turned on the
demonstration of extraordinary individual intellectual promise in fields certain to yield financial return or valuable service to the family. Therefore, a
boy's schooling might extend through high school and beyond only if he
aspired to be a physician, attorney, engineer, dentist, or pharmacist. Lack-
ing aptitude or interest in these professions, he might become a school
teacher, but teaching was a poor substitute in the eyes of parents and was
usually regarded as a choice of last resort (Covello, n.d., folder 17).

Should a boy demonstrate strong ability and desire to prepare for a profession, however, his parents would embrace the idea as a potential boon to
the family and devote everything to the cause of putting him through law
or medical school. Once this process had begun, the same effort that characterized the collective efforts of the family economy would be channeled
toward advancing the boy's career. In return, the boy must affect a serious-
ness of purpose that showed the solemnity of his "bargain" with his family:
he was to focus on his preparation to the exclusion of every possible diver-
sion. His family would provide for him financially even to the extent of
allotting him an allowance, an unheard-of privilege for any other child, boy
or girl (Covello, 1967).

One New Haven man whose parents had emigrated from Campania in
1911 graduated from Hillhouse High School and Yale College before entering Tufts Medical School during the 1920s. While in medical school, he was
spared even the most trivial inconveniences by his family. In addition to
receiving their financial support, he sent his laundry by train from Boston
to New Haven each week for his mother to clean, press, and return to him
by rail the following week (M. Betteti, interview with the author, May 30,
1990). Not all sons anointed for schooling fared so well, of course, and "bit-
terness and disillusionment," according to Covello, was the result "when
high school education proved a blind alley. . . . No government or city job—

no dignified occupation—no status." Much had been sacrificed with nothing gained in recompense. Moreover, the prospect of a son—especially an educated one—who could not support his parents in their old age but instead looked to his parents for assistance after reaching maturity was mortifying. Covello notes the case of "D.T.," who wanted to be a playwright but whose father wanted him to be a doctor. The boy would miss school to go to the library to read dramas and to write, which provoked the father to exclaim, "Am I to spend a fortune in educating this *signorino* so that he can become a *commediante* and bring not only ridicule upon me and my family, but the inevitable of having to support him to the end of my days[?]"(Covello, n.d., folder 17).

Between 1920 and 1930, opposition to girls' schooling began to soften, as did the insistence that boys schooled beyond the minimum enter a profession. These attitudinal changes are captured in high school enrollment rates during the decade. High school attendance, which increased among all groups in New Haven, increased dramatically among children of Italian descent, quadrupling between 1920 and 1930. In part, this is attributable to the opening of a second high school in New Haven in 1920, Commercial High School. Built to meet the demand for the fastest-growing curricular choice of all high school offerings, it fed the expanding market for the female clerical workers and sales clerks. Italian American daughters formed the largest ethnic group in the new high school, and girls outnumbered boys by a wide margin (New Haven Board of Education, 1920–1930; Lassonde, 1994; DeVault, 1990; Rury, 1991; Montgomery, 1987). While the pull of high school was due to the growing demand for clerical workers, which sought both specific skills and the credential of high school, the push into high school came from a concurrent and rapid decline in the demand for adolescent workers. Thus, the age floor of the youth job market was being raised in effect by the disappearance of unskilled jobs in factories that increasingly wanted semiskilled labor (Altenbaugh, 1993).

The Age of Adolescence: From Privilege to Right

Between 1920 and the 1950, high school became the default certifier of a worker's ability to learn new tasks and to adapt readily to new forms of production in the industrial workplace. Despite ill-defined (or unarticulated) reasons for staying in school, those who did remain benefited handsomely in the most general way. Becker (1975) has shown that private rates of return on education after 1939 rewarded high school graduates relatively better than either college graduates or those with fewer than twelve years of school. While private rates of return for college graduates, for instance, remained essentially unchanged from 1940 to 1960, the rate of return for high school graduates rose over the same period by about 75 percent. Although Becker says that the evidence from before 1939 is unreliable, it is believed that the differential rates of return for high school and elementary school graduates widened significantly between the 1920s and the 1950s. Therefore, youths who stayed through high school during the 1920s and 1930s ultimately would be rewarded for their perseverance, even if they had little appreciation at the time of how a high school diploma might pay off down the road (Becker, 1975; Noland and Bakke, 1949).

Judging from the testimony of the second-generation Italian immigrant men interviewed by Child in his classic study of assimilation, *Italian or American?* (1943), it is clear that immigrant parents and youths by the 1920s often regarded the prospect of a high school education from quite different vantage points. Even as extended schooling became a norm in the United States and Italian immigrant parents became less insistent on schooling exclusively for professional preparation, education retained its status as a privilege that could be extended (and, hence, withdrawn) in exchange for the tacit promise by sons of continued compliance with parental wishes until they left home or married. Yet for sons, high school came to represent something closer to a right by the 1920s and 1930s. Failure by parents to honor that right seems more frequently to have resulted in the feeling that a compact had been violated and spawned quiet resentment. The issue arose in several contexts but most pointedly in connection with the practice of turning over one's earnings to parents.

One youth, for instance, reported that he had turned over all of his pay to his parents until he married, despite feeling that he "'wasn't bound to them . . . since they hadn't contributed to . . . [his] education.'" Another youth, who had tried to resist his father's demand to turn over his earnings, eventually capitulated, but he said that when *he* had children one day, he "'would deduct the household expenses for . . . [them and] put the rest of [the] pay in a bank account for their future education'" (Child, 1939, pp. 385–386). Perhaps the experience of another young man best exemplifies the parental view of schooling as a privilege that, when invoked, demanded in return behaviors in keeping with the youth's "dependent" status. He had completed a year of college before finally quitting and noticed that his autonomy at home was compromised whenever he matriculated. A whole range of issues scrutinized by his mother while he was in school—how late he stayed out, with whom he spent his time, how many different girls he dated, how much money he spent—were overlooked when he was contributing to his family's income: "When I'm working," he remarked, "she feels I have more right to do as I want" (Child, 1939, p. 486). In the case of each of these young men, their ability to resist parents' wishes varied widely with respect to choosing between school and work, but they shared the determination to make extended schooling available to their own children when they themselves became parents.

Others merely echoed their parents in posing school and work as alternatives in tension rather than subscribing to the new view of school as an investment in their futures. Another young man, says Child, "spontaneously defended" the custom of turning over his pay to his parents by noting, "My mother gave me the break of letting me go to school and I don't see why I shouldn't give her my pay" (Child, 1939, p. 324). Indeed, many youths who persisted in school for a time under the weight of such ambivalence might be persuaded before long by their neighborhood friends that the cost was too great—that continued submission to parental scrutiny could not be offset by the uncertain rewards of a high school education. Thus, for many children of Italian immigrants, the decision to remain in school was made with the understanding that many of the prerogatives enjoyed by their out-of-school peers would be denied to them as a consequence.

Still other Italian American adolescents, their proportions unknown but their numbers presumably significant, found themselves in high school for lack of any viable alternative. This trend, begun during the 1920s, deepened with the onset of the Great Depression. The raising of the age of compulsory schooling to sixteen in Connecticut in 1932 of course virtually guaranteed that all young people would enter ninth grade. But state surveys of job-seeking youths in the same year revealed that grade attainment had been steadily climbing before the law was passed and that youths were remaining in school in greater numbers beyond grades nine and ten (Connecticut State Employment Service, 1934). Typical of many adolescents was the following attitude summarized by an educational sociologist investigating the variety of motives expressed by youths for staying in school during the mid-1930s: "Case VI—Boy . . . Italian Parentage. Driving force: None. Family indifferent. Boy felt that since there was no job in sight, he might as well stay in school" (Feldman, 1936, p. 171). Common too was a positive valuation of receiving middling grades, especially among boys (Fass, 1977; Modell and Alexander, 1997). Although girls in all tracks generally worried more about not earning poor grades, many boys in what was called the general course of study felt that it was downright dishonorable to earn anything better than a C. As one boy put it, "C is just right because it's not high nor low." Another student stated that an average mark is good, "because it's passing and [I] cannot afford to go to college so I'll have to work when I leave school anyway." A third elaborated on this rationale even further, declaring that he could do better than a C but that he "didn't feel much like it . . . [because] it doesn't always get you where you want to go. Take college students for example, you see a lot of them just digging didges [sic]. You take a high school graduate and he'll have a better job than the other fellow" (Nordli, 1942, p. 71). The new indifference toward the reward system of high school offers ironic testimony to the degree to which remaining in school had become the normal experience of American adolescents.

Conclusion

Between 1920 and 1930, enrollment in New Haven's high schools increased by more than 50 percent. Although New Haven's Italian immigrant population began to level off during the 1920s, the enrollment of

Italian American youths in the city's two high schools increased dramatically during this period. In 1920, the sons and daughters of Italian-born parents were fewer than one in ten high school students; by 1930, one in five Hillhouse High School students was of Italian descent, and one in four Commercial High School pupils was of Italian origin (New Haven Board of Education, 1900–1932). A new high-water mark had been reached in secondary schooling, and Italian immigrant parents capitulated to the determination (or, just as often, the resignation) of their children to trudge off to high school instead of to the factory, in the face of diminishing opportunities for them to contribute to the family economy.

The verso of this trend—whether driven by determination *or* resignation—was the growing acceptance during the 1930s of a developmental view of children's age-appropriate readiness to assume adult-like responsibilities in New Haven's Italian immigrant families. High school was both a cultural marker in this sense—an emblem of the adoption of adolescence as a meaningful phase in the child's preparation for adult life—and the site of immigrant children's accommodation to the occupational system of American capitalism. The second-generation Italian immigrant men interviewed by Irvin Child aptly represent the transition to this new view in describing their struggles with parents to win what many had come to believe was their right to attend high school. This assertion symbolized a historic renegotiation of children's and parents' obligations to one another in the family wage economy of southern Italian immigrants—one mediated thereafter by parents' grudging acceptance of high school attendance and adolescence as the prerogative of American-born children.

References

Altenbaugh, R. J. "Families, Children, Schools, and the Workplace." In S. W. Rothstein (ed.), *Handbook of Schooling in Urban America*. Westport, Conn.: Greenwood Press, 1993.

Banfield, E. C. *The Moral Basis of a Backward Society*. New York: Free Press, 1958.

Barton, J. J. *Peasants and Strangers: Italians, Rumanians, and Slovaks in an American City, 1890–1950*. Cambridge, Mass.: Harvard University Press, 1975.

Becker, G. S. *Human Capital: A Theoretical and Empirical Analysis, with Special Reference to Education*. New York: Columbia University Press, 1975.

Bell, R. M. *Fate and Honor, Family and Village: Demographic and Cultural Change in Rural Italy Since 1800*. Chicago: University of Chicago Press, 1979.

Bodnar, J. "Immigration, Kinship, and the Rise of Working-Class Realism." *Journal of Social History,* 1980, *14,* 45–66.

Child, I. L. "A Psychological Study of Second-Generation Italians." Unpublished doctoral dissertation, Yale University, 1939.

Child, I. L. *Italian or American? The Second Generation in Conflict*. New Haven, Conn.: Yale University Press, 1943.

Chudacoff, H. P. *How Old Are You? Age Consciousness in American Culture*. Princeton, N.J.: Princeton University Press, 1989.

Clubb, J. M., Austin, E. W., and Kirk, G. W., Jr. *The Process of Historical Inquiry: Everyday Lives of Working Americans*. New York: Columbia University Press, 1989.

Cohen, M. *Workshop to Office: Two Generations of Italian Women in New York City, 1900–1950.* Ithaca, N.Y.: Cornell University Press, 1992.

Cole, M., and Cole, S. R. *The Development of Children.* (3rd ed.) New York: Freeman, 1996.

Connecticut State Employment Service. *Youths in Search of Jobs!* Hartford: Connecticut State Employment Service, 1934.

Covello, L. *The Social Background of the Italo-American School Child: A Study of the Southern Italian Family Mores and Their Effect on the School Situation in Italy and America.* Leiden, Netherlands: E. J. Brill, 1967.

Covello, Leonard, Collection. Research Library of the Balch Institute for Ethnic Studies, Philadelphia. MSS 40, box 66. N.d.

Cutts, N. E. "The Extent of Bilingualism and Its Effect on Beginning Reading in a Group of First Year Children Largely of Italian Parentage." Unpublished doctoral dissertation, Yale University, 1933.

DeVault, I. A. *Sons and Daughters of Labor: Class and Clerical Work in Turn-of-the-Century Pittsburgh.* Ithaca, N.Y.: Cornell University Press, 1990.

Fass, P. S. *The Damned and the Beautiful: American Youth in the 1920s.* New York: Oxford University Press, 1977.

Feldman, E. E. "The Dull Child and the Junior High Curriculum." Unpublished doctoral dissertation, Yale University, 1936.

Glenn, S. A. *Daughters of the Shtetl: Life and Labor in the Immigrant Generation.* Ithaca, N.Y.: Cornell University Press, 1990.

Hogan, D. J. "Education and the Making of the Chicago Working Class, 1880–1930." *History of Education Quarterly,* 1978, *18,* 227–270.

Kett, J. F. *Rites of Passage: Adolescence in America, 1790 to the Present.* New York: Basic Books, 1977.

Lassonde, S. A. "Learning to Forget: Schooling and Family Life in New Haven's Working Class, 1870–1940." Unpublished doctoral dissertation, Yale University, 1994.

Lassonde, S. "Learning and Earning: Schooling, Juvenile Employment, and the Early Life Course in Late Nineteenth-Century New Haven." *Journal of Social History,* 1996, *29,* 839–870.

Levine, D. *Reproducing Families: The Political Economy of English Population History.* Cambridge, England: Cambridge University Press, 1987.

Mead, M. *Coming of Age in Samoa: A Psychological Study of Primitive Youth for Western Civilisation.* New York: Morrow, 1928.

Mirel, J. E. "Twentieth-Century America, Adolescence." In R. M. Lerner, A. C. Peterson, and J. Brooks-Gunn (eds.), *Encyclopedia of Adolescence.* New York: Garland, 1991.

Modell, J. "Patterns of Consumption, Acculturation, and Family Income Strategies in Late Nineteenth-Century America." In T. K. Hareven and M. A. Vinovskis (eds.), *Family and Population in Nineteenth-Century America.* Princeton, N.J.: Princeton University Press, 1978.

Modell, J., and Alexander, J. T. "High School in Transition: Community, School, and Peer Group in Abilene, Kansas, 1939." *History of Education Quarterly,* 1997, *3,* 1–24.

Montgomery, D. *Fall of the House of Labor: The Workplace, the State, and American Labor Activism, 1865–1925.* Cambridge, England: Cambridge University Press, 1987.

Myers, J. K. "The Differential Time Factor in Assimilation." Unpublished doctoral dissertation, Yale University, 1950.

New Haven Board of Education. *Annual Report.* New Haven, Conn.: Tuttle, Morehouse & Co., 1870–1932.

Noland, W. E., and Bakke, E. W. *Workers Wanted: A Study of Employers' Hiring Policies, Preferences, and Practices in New Haven and Charlotte.* New York: HarperCollins, 1949.

Nordli, W. "Rewards and Punishments of High School Students." Unpublished doctoral dissertation, Yale University, 1942.

Olneck, M. R., and Lazerson, M. "The School Achievement of Immigrant Children: 1900–1930." *History of Education Quarterly,* 1974, *14,* 453–482.

Orsi, R. A. *The Madonna of 115th Street: Faith and Community in Italian Harlem, 1880–1950.* New Haven, Conn.: Yale University Press, 1985.

Perlmann, J. *Ethnic Differences: Schooling and Social Structure Among the Irish, Italians, Jews, and Blacks in an American City, 1880–1935.* Cambridge, England: Cambridge University Press, 1988.

Racca, V. "Ethnography: The Italians of New Haven." WPA, Federal Writers' Project, Connecticut Ethnic Survey. University of Connecticut, Storrs, box 67, folder 175:3, n.d.

Racca, V. "Selected Family Histories." Manuscripts and Archives, Sterling Memorial Library, Yale University, YRG-37, box 37, folder 288, n.d.

Rury, J. L. *Education and Women's Work: Female Schooling and the Division of Labor in Urban America, 1870–1930.* Albany: State University of New York Press, 1991.

Smith, J. E. *Family Connections: A History of Italian and Jewish Immigrant Lives in Providence, Rhode Island, 1900–1940.* Albany: State University of New York Press, 1985.

Smith, T. L. "Immigrant Social Aspirations and American Education, 1880–1930." *American Quarterly,* 1969, 21, 523–543.

Thernstrom, S. *Poverty and Progress: Social Mobility in a Nineteenth Century City.* Cambridge, Mass.: Harvard University Press, 1964.

Vecoli, R. J. "Prelates and Peasants: Italian Immigrants and the Catholic Church." *Journal of Social History,* 1969, 2, 217–268.

Whitelaw, J. B. "The Administration of the Elementary School as the Coordinating Social Factor in the Community." Unpublished doctoral dissertation, Yale University, 1935.

Williams, P. H. *South Italian Folkways in Europe and America.* New Haven, Conn.: Yale University Press, 1938.

Yans-McLaughlin, V. *Family and Community: Italian Immigrants in Buffalo, 1880–1930.* Ithaca, N.Y.: Cornell University Press, 1977.

STEPHEN LASSONDE is a lecturer in history at Yale University, New Haven, Connecticut.

4

A sense of obligation to the family is associated with a greater belief in the importance and usefulness of education and accounts for the tendency of Asian and Latin American adolescents to have greater academic motivation than their equally achieving peers with European backgrounds.

Family Obligation and the Academic Motivation of Adolescents from Asian, Latin American, and European Backgrounds

Andrew J. Fuligni

Asian and Latin American families in the United States have been often characterized as placing a greater importance on familial duty and obligation than families with European backgrounds do. Many traditions within Asian cultures, such as Confucianism, emphasize family solidarity, respect, and commitment (Ho, 1981; Shon and Ja, 1982; Uba, 1994). Within Latin American cultures, devotion and loyalty to family is often an imperative for individuals (Chilman, 1993). Family members in traditional Asian and Latin American cultures are expected to support each other and assist in the maintenance in the household. The needs of the family usually have priority, and individual members often are asked to downplay their own needs and desires if they conflict with those of the larger group. In American society, these cultural traditions take on immediate and practical importance because the immigrant and minority statuses of most Asian and Latin American families create the very real need for family members to support one another (Fuligni, 1998).

In our research, my colleagues and I have found that adolescents from Asian and Latin American backgrounds in the United States quickly internalize their families' traditions of family support and respect (Fuligni, Tseng,

Support for the preparation of this chapter and the research it describes has been provided by a Faculty Scholars Award from the William T. Grant Foundation and a FIRST Award from the National Institute of Child Health and Human Development.

and Lam, 1999). As compared to their peers from European backgrounds, Chinese, Filipino, Mexican, and Central and South American youths all believe that they should spend more time doing things such as taking care of their siblings, helping out around the house, assisting their parents at work and in official tasks (such as dealing with government offices), and spending time with the family. Asian and Latin American teenagers are also more likely to believe that they should make sacrifices for the family and take into account the wishes of the family when making important decisions about their own lives. Finally, these youths tend to believe that such obligations to their families exist throughout their lives; they do not diminish as the youths themselves become adults. Interestingly, we have observed that these values remain strong across different generations of youths. Adolescents from immigrant and American-born families share many of the same ideas regarding their familial duties. The only difference that we have observed is a greater tendency for youths from immigrant families to believe that such duties are lifelong obligations, but even adolescents from American-born Asian and Latin American families endorse such a belief more strongly than their European American peers do.

Although discussions of filial duties usually focus on children's assistance with chores or sibling care, children's obligations to the family can also extend to activities outside the household. In particular, Asian and Latin American adolescents in the United States often view school success as one of the most important ways that they can assist their families. Asian and Latin American parents often emigrate to the United States in order to provide their children with better opportunities, including the chance to pursue education through and even beyond secondary school. Ethnographers report that some students say that they would feel guilty about not trying hard in school, given the many personal and professional sacrifices their parents made to come to this country (Caplan, Choy, and Whitmore, 1991; Suárez-Orozco and Suárez-Orozco, 1995). Other adolescents believe that their educational attainment will help them to secure employment and support the family in the future. Students from Asian and Latin American families often cite such indebtedness and responsibility as their primary motivations to do well in school (Zhou and Bankston, 1998). These themes suggest that adolescents' obligation to their family may be connected to a specific belief in the usefulness of education for both their and their families' futures. Rather than enhancing students' intrinsic interest in education in and of itself, familial duty may create a belief that education is important because it provides a means to a valued end.

The family obligation of children from Asian and Latin American families, and its connection to educational attainment, may have important implications for the academic motivation and behavior of these children during adolescence. Indeed, numerous studies have documented that Asian and Latin American youths tend to be either equally or even more motivated than their European American peers during secondary school. Our findings have been consistent with most other studies (Fuligni, 1997). Asian American adolescents, particularly those from Chinese backgrounds, tend to report the strongest values of school success, the highest educational aspirations, and the greatest amount of time spent studying for tests and doing homework after school. Latin American adolescents, despite having done relatively worse in school than their peers for many years, manage to maintain levels of motivation and effort that are approximately equal to those of students from European backgrounds.

To what extent may these ethnic variations in academic motivation be attributable to a sense of family obligation among youths from Asian and Latin American backgrounds? In earlier analyses, we did observe that adolescents' attitudes toward family obligation were associated with individual differences in academic motivation (Fuligni and Tseng, 1999). In the analyses described in this chapter, we clarify and expand on those findings by addressing three specific questions. First, is the link between family obligation and academic motivation specific to a belief in the utility of education, in contrast to an intrinsic interest in academics? Second, are the ethnic differences in motivation also specific to beliefs in the importance and usefulness of education? Given the first two questions, our third question is, Can ethnic variations in academic motivation be attributable to a strong sense of duty and obligation to the family on the part of Asian and Latin American youths? The answers to all three questions were in the affirmative. In particular, we found that a sense of duty and obligation to the family can explain some of the ethnic variations in academic motivation during secondary school, and in a complex way that could have significant implications for the future educational persistence of these youths.

A Longitudinal Study of Adolescents from Asian, Latin American, and European Backgrounds

For the past several years, we have been conducting a longitudinal study of the normative development of approximately one thousand adolescents from immigrant and native-born families with Asian, Latin American, and European backgrounds. The study began when the adolescents were in junior high school and continues to this day as the youths are in the midst of making the transition from adolescence to young adulthood. The youths in our study attended school in an ethnically diverse district in the San Francisco Bay Area that includes a large number of immigrant families. Over 85 percent of the students in our study came from Latin American (Mexican, Central and South American), East Asian (predominantly Chinese), Filipino, and European backgrounds. Overall, approximately two-thirds of the students had at least one foreign-born parent; the remainder came from families in which both parents were born in the United States. The distribution of immigrant and American-born families varied across ethnic backgrounds, such that the majority of all but those from European backgrounds had foreign-born parents. The adolescents also varied in terms of their socioeconomic background. Students from

East Asian and Filipino families had parents with the highest educational and occupational levels, whereas those from Latin American families had parents with the lowest levels of education and occupation.

As part of the study, adolescents completed questionnaires that tapped their beliefs and values regarding the family and education. The students' year-end grades in their courses were obtained from official school records.

Ethnic Differences in Family Obligations

After conducting a series of focus groups in which we discussed various aspects of youth's duties and obligations to their families, we created a set of questions that assessed adolescents' attitudes toward three types of family obligations. The first, which we called *current assistance*, referred to the degree to which adolescents believed that they should assist with household tasks and help the family. Youths indicated how often they felt they should engage in activities such as run errands for the family, help out around the house, take care of brothers and sisters, and spend time with other family members. The second type of obligation was called *family respect*. Students were asked to evaluate the importance of respecting parents and older family members, doing well for the sake of the family, and making sacrifices for the family. The final aspect of family obligations that we assessed involved the value the students placed on *supporting the family in the future*. Youths indicated how important they believed it was to help their parents financially in the future, live or go to college near their parents, and help take care of their parents and other family members in the future. All three scales were highly reliable, with alpha coefficients well above .70 for the various ethnic groups.

As we reported previously (Fuligni, Tseng, and Lam, 1999), adolescents from Asian and Latin American families endorsed all three aspects of family obligations more strongly than did the youths from European backgrounds. Chinese, Filipino, Mexican, and Central and South American youths believed that they should assist and spend time with their family, respect their parents' wishes and make sacrifices for their family, and support their family in the future more than did their European American peers. These differences tended to be large, sometimes reaching more than a full standard deviation in magnitude, and could not be accounted for by ethnic variations in socioeconomic status and family composition (such as family size and the presence of grandparents). Given these findings, we felt that we were tapping a value and tradition that was strongly associated with the youths' ethnic and cultural background.

Family Obligation and Academic Motivation

We assessed several different aspects of the students' attitudes toward school in order to examine the link between family obligation and academic motivation. To tap the students' value of academic success, adolescents were asked to rate the importance of outcomes such as, "Doing well in school," "Being one of the best students in your class," and "Going to college after high school." Adolescents' perceptions of the future utility of education were measured by having students respond to statements such as, "Going to college is necessary for what I want to do in the future," "I need to get good grades in school to get a good job as an adult," and "Doing well in school is the best way for me to succeed as an adult." Finally, we assessed two different components of adolescents' subject-specific values of mathematics and English using scales developed by Eccles and her colleagues (Eccles, 1983). The first component, the intrinsic value of the subjects, included the items, "In general, I find working on math [English] assignments interesting" and "How much do you like math [English]?" The second component tapped more of a utility value of the subjects and included questions such as, "In the future, how useful do you think math [English] will be in your everyday life?" and "How useful do you think math [English] will be for what you want to be after you graduate from school and go to work?" All of the scales were highly reliable, with internal consistencies well above .70 and .80.

Correlational analyses were conducted in order to determine whether a sense of family obligation was related to academic motivation. These correlations demonstrate a notable and consistent link between an emphasis on assistance to the family and a value of academic achievement. As shown in the first two rows of Table 4.1, adolescents who believed that they should assist, support, and respect their family placed a stronger value on achieving a measure of academic success and going on to college. These youths also had a stronger belief in the utility and importance of schooling for their future occupational successes as adults.

The two components of the subject-specific measures enabled us to compare the implications of family obligation for a belief in the utility of education with the implications for a more intrinsic interest in academics. If family obligation is indeed more salient for a belief in the usefulness of education, it should be more highly correlated with youths' utility values of math and English than with the youths' intrinsic values. We first partialed out the variance that the intrinsic value and utility value shared with one another so that we could assess the independent associations of the values with family obligation. As shown in Table 4.1, adolescents' sense of family obligation was more strongly related to the their belief in the usefulness of math and English than it was to how much they liked the subjects. These results suggest that adolescents' sense of obligation does not have a global and indiscriminate association with their education-related attitudes and beliefs. Rather, the link appears to be specific to a higher value of the importance and utility of academic endeavors. Additional analyses not reported here indicated that correlations were similar across the different ethnic groups, suggesting that a sense of family obligation is associated with greater academic motivation even among cultural groups for whom the tradition is relatively less important.

Table 4.1. Correlations Between Adolescents' Attitudes Toward Family Obligation and Their Academic Values

	Current Assistance (r)	Family Respect (r)	Future Support (r)
Value of academic success	.33	.40	.28
Utility of education	.26	.33	.22
Utility value of math	.20	.28	.22
Utility value of English	.16	.18	.16
Intrinsic value of math	.04	.05	.00
Intrinsic value of English	.03	−.07	−.08

Note: All correlations except for those with intrinsic values are significant at $p < .001$. Correlations for the math and English values are partial correlations, in which the shared variance between utility and intrinsic values has been removed.

Given the longitudinal nature of our study, we can go beyond these correlations and examine the extent to which a sense of family obligation is associated with changes in adolescents' academic motivation over time. That is, do adolescents who believe in the importance of assisting and supporting their families follow different developmental trajectories of academic motivation over time? As shown in Figure 4.1, the answer is yes. Between the sixth and eighth grades, the time that covers the transition from elementary to middle school in this school district, little difference in the academic value of adolescents exists according to their sense of family obligation. In addition, there is no decline in academic motivation for any of these students during this period. The transition to high school is associated with a rapid decline in the value of academic success that continues throughout the high school years. This decline, however, is notably and significantly less steep for students with a strong sense of duty to support and assist their families. We see virtually the same pattern when we examine the longitudinal trends in the other aspects of academic motivation. Students with a sense of family obligation apparently cannot avoid the increased disenchantment with education that is so prevalent among American high school students, but the youths are able to complete secondary school with a higher value of academic success than their peers.

In summary, adolescents who more strongly believed that they should assist, support, and respect the family also placed more importance on the importance of being successful in school and going on to college. These youths also believed in the usefulness of both education in general and their math and English classes in particular for their future lives and occupational careers. In contrast, a sense of family obligation was not associated with more intrinsic interest in academics. Youths with a strong sense of familial duty did not like their academic subjects any more. They were equal to their peers in terms of their intrinsic motivation while greater in

Figure 4.1. Changes in the Value of Academic Success During Secondary School According to Level of Family Obligation

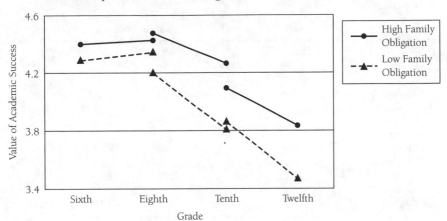

terms of their utility motivation. In addition to being associated with a greater instrumental type of educational motivation, family obligation appeared to ameliorate the dramatic declines in adolescents' engagement with school that takes place during the secondary school years.

Ethnic Differences in Academic Motivation

Given the connection between youths' sense of family obligation and their belief in the importance of education, do we find ethnic variations in academic motivation that parallel the ethnic differences in family obligation? The answer to this question is yes, but the findings suggest that obligation plays a role in a rather complicated and interesting way.

As shown in Table 4.2, we find ethnic variations in academic motivation that mirror those found in most other studies, but with a twist. First, Asian adolescents (those with Chinese and Filipino backgrounds) consistently report the highest level of academic motivation. These youths place more importance succeeding in school and going on to college, and they have stronger faith in the importance and utility of education for their adult lives as compared to those from European backgrounds. The differences between the Latin American and European American students are less consistent, but the Mexican and Central and South American students do indicate a value of academic success and a belief in the utility of education that is either equal to or greater than their peers from European backgrounds.

The twist in Table 4.2 is in the ethnic differences in the utility values of math and English as compared with the intrinsic values. Asian, and to some degree Latin American, students report a stronger belief in the importance and usefulness of these two school subjects as compared with European American

Table 4.2. Ethnic Differences in Adolescents' Academic Values

	Chinese (M)	Filipino (M)	Mexican (M)	Central and South American (M)	European (M)
Value of academic success	4.17[a]	4.09[a]	3.56	3.76[a]	3.45
Utility of education	4.59[a]	4.53[a]	4.17[a]	4.26[a]	3.99
Utility value of math	4.07[a]	4.08[a]	3.91[a]	4.02[a]	3.57
Utility value of English	4.49[a]	4.30[a]	3.89	4.13	3.96
Intrinsic value of math	3.03	3.02	2.77	2.59	2.86
Intrinsic value of English	2.84	3.05	3.04	3.18	3.16

Note: All values were measured on a five-point scale; a higher value indicates a stronger value.

[a]Indicates a group mean that is significantly different from the European group mean at $p < .05$ or less. Means for math and English values are adjusted means in which the shared variance between utility and intrinsic values has been removed.

students. In contrast, there are no differences in the adolescents' intrinsic value of math and English, which is the extent to which the youths like the subjects and find them interesting. It is important to note that the Asian and Latin American students do not like the subjects any more than their European American peers do. All youths demonstrate an approximately equal level of intrinsic motivation in these subjects. The pattern of results for the utility and intrinsic values supports the hypothesis that ethnic differences in academic motivation during adolescence have more to do with a stronger belief in the importance and utility of education among Asian and Latin American students than with any variation in the intrinsic value and pleasure the youths obtain from their academic endeavors.

How do the ethnic variations in motivation map onto the ethnic differences in family obligation that we observed earlier? The high level of academic motivation on the part of the Asian adolescents is consistent with their strong sense of family obligation. But the Latin American youths do not report as consistent and as a high a level of academic motivation that would have been expected from their strong sense of duty and obligation to the family. In an effort to understand this apparent discrepancy in findings, we looked at the students' actual performance in school. Adolescents from Chinese backgrounds receive the highest grades in school, followed by those with Filipino and European backgrounds, who achieve at an approximately equal level. Latin American students, including both those with Mexican and Central and South American backgrounds, tend to receive the lowest grades in school (Fuligni, 1997).

These differences in achievement, observed in virtually all studies of secondary school performance, are not attributable to the ethnic differences in family obligation. There is no linear association between a sense of family obligation and adolescents' academic achievement. After we control for youths' sense of family obligation, Chinese students still receive the highest grades, and Latin American students still receive the lowest (Fuligni, Tseng, and Lam, 1999). Rather than being due to family obligation, these ethnic differences are more strongly related to factors in the youths' socioeconomic background, such as parental educational level and language use in the home (Fuligni, 1997).

Why should these differences in actual achievement at school play a role in the link between family obligation and ethnic variations in motivation? The link between motivation and achievement can be reciprocal: higher motivation can lead to better performance in school, but lower grades can also erode students' motivation over time. Given the reciprocal effects between motivation and performance, which we do observe in our study, the question should not be, Why isn't the motivation of the Latin American students higher? Rather, the question should be, Why is their motivation so high despite receiving such low grades in school? Similarly, why is the motivation of the Filipino students higher than that of European American students despite achieving a similar level of performance?

These conditional differences in adolescents' value of academic success, controlling for the youths' academic achievement, are shown in Figure 4.2. This figure shows the differences in the value of academic success between the Asian and Latin American adolescents and their equally achieving European American peers. Representing the contrast between the ethnic differences in motivation and the ethnic differences in achievement, this chart shows that adolescents from Asian and Latin American families report a significantly higher value of academic success than do European American students who attain the same level of performance in school.

It is this tendency for adolescents from Asian and Latin American backgrounds to place more emphasis on the importance and utility of education as compared to their equally achieving European American peers that seems to be associated with a sense of duty to support and assist the family. When we control for the sense of family obligation, the ethnic differences in motivation become significantly reduced (see Figure 4.3). This significant statistical mediation suggests that the desire for Asian and Latin American students to support, assist, and respect their families leads them to place more value on the importance and usefulness of education than do their European American peers who are achieving a similar level of performance in school.

Ethnic differences in the developmental trends in adolescents' academic value, conditional on grade point average, are shown in Figure 4.4. All youths experience declines in their academic values, but the declines are slightly and significantly less steep for the youths from Asian and Latin American

Figure 4.2. Differences in the Value of Academic Success Between Asian and Latin American Adolescents and Their Equally Achieving European American Peers

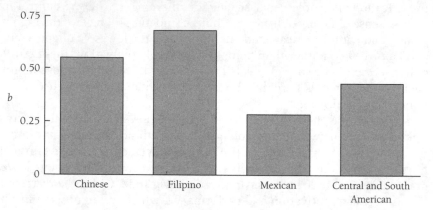

Note: Each bar represents the difference in values between a specific Asian or Latin American group and their equally achieving European American peers. Differences were estimated using dummy variable regressions, controlling for grade point average, with European American students as the baseline. All differences are significant at $p < .01$ or less.

Figure 4.3. Differences in the Value of Academic Success Between Asian and Latin American Adolescents and Their Equally Achieving European American Peers, Controlling for Family Obligation

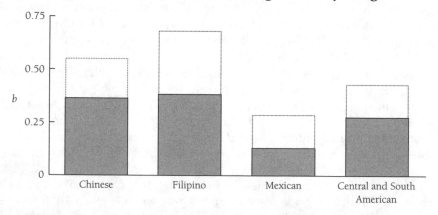

Note: White areas represent the amount of the original ethnic differences that were associated with adolescents' attitudes toward family obligations. Shaded areas represent the amount of differences remaining after controlling for family obligations.

Figure 4.4. Ethnic Differences in the Changes in the Value of Academic Success Among Equally Achieving Adolescents During Secondary School

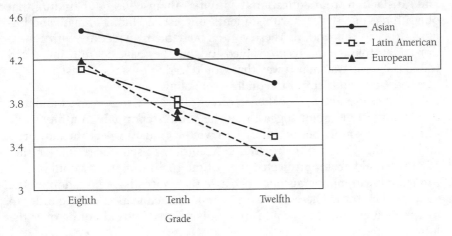

Note: Means have been adjusted for adolescents' grade point average.

backgrounds. There is a cross-over between the youths from Latin American and European backgrounds such that the students from Latin American families finish high school years with a slightly higher level of academic motivation than their equally achieving European American peers. As with the mean differences in motivation shown in Figures 4.2 and 4.3, these ethnic differences in the developmental changes in motivation can also be explained by variations in family obligation. When we control for adolescents' sense of family obligation, the divergence between the different groups reduces and the lines become more parallel.

In summary, Asian and Latin American adolescents tend to place more value on the importance and usefulness of education for their future lives than their equally achieving European American counterparts. In contrast, youths from the different ethnic backgrounds did not differ in terms of their intrinsic academic motivation. Ethnic differences in adolescents' sense of family obligation played a significant role in the tendency for Asian and Latin American youths to want to do better and go further in school than their equally achieving peers from European backgrounds.

Conclusion

What is the significance of what appears to be an obligation-based belief in the importance and utility of education for the eventual educational attainment of youths from Asian and Latin American backgrounds? Some current models of motivation might actually predict a limited effect on attainment. Self-determination theory (Deci and Ryan, 1985; Grolnik, Deci, and Ryan, 1997) might expect a small effect because an obligation-based utility value of education may not be fully intrinsic to the adolescents. That is, a student who believes in the importance of education because it could help the family is not necessarily pursuing education because he or she derives pleasure and satisfaction from educational activities themselves. Our finding that obligation is unassociated with students' interest and liking of math and English supports this notion. These youths therefore may identify with education and its role as a means to a valued end, but they have not fully integrated it into their self-system in a way that would lead to the task persistence necessary to go far in their postsecondary schooling.

Even worse, the links between our measure of family respect and academic motivation might suggest that the youths report a high utility value of education simply because they believe they must respect the authority and obey the wishes of their parents. According to self-determination theory, this would be an introjected type of internalization that would lead to limited educational persistence because the youths have not adopted the value as their own. These adolescents believe in education only in order to please their parents and would likely disengage from schooling over the long term.

Similarly, work on approach-avoidance motivations might expect the obligation-related motivation to be less conducive to long-term educational persistence (Elliot, 1999). It may be that the value of education among those with a sense of familial duty may be more of an avoidance motivation, in which the adolescents believe that they must persist educationally in order to avoid the consequences of not doing so. These consequences could range from a bleak economic future for the family to a sense of shame and dishonor because of disappointing one's parents and family. An avoidance motivation can be contrasted to an approach motivation, where youths would endorse the utility of education for what it offers rather than for what it prevents.

In actuality, it is difficult to make predictions using these two perspectives without obtaining additional information about the youths' sense of obligation to the family and educational motivation. For example, we do not know whether adolescents who endorse their family obligations do so because it is a fully integrated and accepted part of their general system of values, or whether it stems from a desire to please their parents and families. Similarly, it is unclear in our research whether youths endorse the importance of assisting and respecting the family because they truly hold that cultural value or because they are afraid of the consequences of not fulfilling such duties (for example, family disapproval and estrangement). These issues are similarly unclear in terms of the youths' academic motivation. It is important in the next phase of our research to tap these additional dimensions of youths' sense of family obligation and academic motivation in order to understand their implications for long-term development.

Yet even without having this additional information, we hazard the prediction that at the individual level, a belief in the utility of education that is rooted in youths' sense of family obligation will lead to greater postsecondary educational persistence. We make this prediction because there was no evidence that students with a sense of family obligation had lower intrinsic motivation. That is, students who believed that they should assist and respect the authority of the family found their academic subjects just as interesting and enjoyable as those with a lower sense of familial duty. Given the similar level of intrinsic motivation, the greater belief in the importance and usefulness of education should lead those with a sense of family obligation to go further in school than their peers. Some evidence does exist that a utility value can predict persistence above and beyond an intrinsic value, especially during adolescence. Wigfield and Eccles (1989) found that high schoolers' perception of the usefulness of mathematics had an association with the students' intention to continue taking math, independent of the youths' interest and liking of the subject.

For the same reasons, the greater sense of obligation among those with Asian and Latin American backgrounds may lead them to greater educational persistence as compared to their equally achieving peers from European backgrounds. The prediction for the Asian American youths is not surprising, given their generally high rate of college attendance. We believe, however, that not all of the difference between Asian American and other youths in postsecondary schooling will be attributable to their high level of academic performance during high school. It is possible that part of the difference will be due to an obligation-based belief in the importance and usefulness of education.

The prediction for the Latin American youths is more difficult, as they tend to have lower rates of educational attainment overall. Yet in comparison to European American students with the same level of academic achievement during high school, youths from Latin American backgrounds may persist further because of their desire to support, assist, and respect the family. There is some evidence that under certain conditions, members of lower-achieving minority groups may go further in school than their equally achieving European American peers. Bowen and Bock (1998), in their study of African American students admitted to prestigious colleges, found that whereas these students received lower grades in school than European American students, they were more likely to pursue graduate degrees when compared with their equally achieving peers. Given the lower level of academic performance of Latin American students, their overall educational attainment is not likely to be high. But compared with equally achieving peers from European American backgrounds, the Latin American students may show evidence of greater postsecondary persistence by attending a community college or specialized training school.

Finally, family obligation may lead to educational persistence among Asian and Latin American students because a belief in the importance of education that is rooted in a tradition of family support and respect may be just as strong as a more purely intrinsic motivation among European American youths. Several observers have suggested that a collectivistic orientation such as family obligation may lead to motivations that are more strongly based on one's social identity and connection to the group (Markus and Kitayama, 1991). Given the importance of family obligation within Asian and Latin American families, a motivation that is tied to that cultural norm could have an effect on long-term task persistence that is similar to a more individualistic, intrinsic motivation among European American youths.

In conclusion, whether the family-based motivation of the adolescents from Asian and Latin American families leads to greater persistence and perhaps educational attainment remains to be seen. The economic realities faced by the youths' families will be a powerful force in shaping their future educational and occupational decisions, as will the possible gender-based demands of the family and the youths' actual performance in school. As we continue to follow the youths in our study as they make their transition to adulthood, we expect to observe a rich variety of strategies by which youths with a sense of familial duty and obligation balance the immediate needs of their families with their attempts to receive enough schooling in order to ensure their families' long-term economic stability.

References

Bowen, W. G., and Bock, D. *The Shape of the River: Long-Term Consequences of Considering Race in College and University Admissions.* Princeton, N.J.: Princeton University Press, 1998.

Caplan, N., Choy, M. H., and Whitmore, J. K. *Children of the Boat People: A Study of Educational Success.* Ann Arbor: University of Michigan Press, 1991.

Chilman, C. S. "Hispanic Families in the United States: Research Perspectives." In H. P. McAdoo (ed.), *Family Ethnicity: Strength in Diversity.* Thousand Oaks, Calif.: Sage, 1993.

Deci, E. L., and Ryan, R. M. *Intrinsic Motivation and Self-Determination in Human Behavior.* New York: Plenum Press, 1985.

Eccles, J. S. "Expectancies, Values, and Academic Behaviors." In J. T. Spence (ed.), *Achievement and Achievement Motivation.* New York: Freeman, 1983.

Elliot, A. "Approach and Avoidance Motivation and Achievement Goals." *Educational Psychologist, 1999, 34,* 169–189.

Fuligni, A. J. "The Academic Achievement of Adolescents from Immigrant Families: The Roles of Family Background, Attitudes, and Behavior." *Child Development, 1997, 68,* 261–273.

Fuligni, A. J. "The Adjustment of Children from Immigrant Families." *Current Directions in Psychological Science, 1998, 7,* 99–103.

Fuligni, A. J., and Tseng, V. "Family Obligations and the Achievement Motivation of Children from Immigrant and American-Born Families." In T. Urdan (ed.), *Advances in Motivation and Achievement.* Greenwich, Conn.: JAI Press, 1999.

Fuligni, A. J., Tseng, V., and Lam, M. "Attitudes Toward Family Obligations Among American Adolescents from Asian, Latin American, and European Backgrounds." *Child Development, 1999, 70,* 1030–1044.

Grolnik, W. S., Deci, E. L., and Ryan, R. M. "Internalization Within the Family: The Self-Determination Theory Perspective." In J. E. Grusek and L. Kuczynski (eds.), *Parenting and Children's Internalization of Values.* New York: Wiley, 1997.

Ho, D.Y.F. "Traditional Patterns of Socialization in Chinese Society." *Acta Psychologica Taiwanica, 1981, 23,* 81–95.

Markus, H. R., and Kitayama, S. "Culture and the Self: Implications for Cognition, Emotion, and Motivation." *Psychological Review, 1991, 98,* 224–253.

Shon, S. P., and Ja, D. Y. "Asian Families." In M. McGoldrick, J. K. Pearce, and J. Giordano (eds.), *Ethnicity and Family Therapy*. New York: Guilford Press, 1982.

Suárez-Orozco, C., and Suárez-Orozco, M. M. *Transformations: Immigration, Family Life, and Achievement Motivation Among Latino Adolescents*. Stanford, Calif.: Stanford University Press, 1995.

Uba, L. *Asian Americans: Personality Patterns, Identity, and Mental Health*. New York: Guilford Press, 1994.

Wigfield, A., and Eccles, J. S. "Relations of Expectancies and Values to Students' Math Grades and Intentions." Paper presented at the meeting of the American Educational Research Association, San Francisco, 1989.

Zhou, M., and Bankston, C. L. *Growing Up American: How Vietnamese Children Adapt to Life in the United States*. New York: Russell Sage Foundation, 1998.

ANDREW J. FULIGNI is associate professor of psychology at New York University.

5

Family obligation and assistance are fundamental features of children's development that link general developmental processes with the context of a particular historical moment and a specific cultural community.

Children Investing in Their Families: The Importance of Child Obligation in Successful Development

Thomas S. Weisner

Development is organized by engaged participation by children in the activities they find in daily life. The psychological experiences of children and youth are mutually made up by the sociocultural worlds they encounter and live within, as well as by processes of the human mind. To understand children's roles in a system of family obligation and assistance, then, we need to know what children do in those activities in order to know what they think and feel, just as much as we need to know about obligation from the other way around—the more common way in psychology—which is to study what children feel and think in order to understand what they do. Kessen (1993) reminded developmentalists that understanding and explaining what children do should be at the core of what we want to know about children and families, yet for reasons of method, theory, and disciplinarity, we have somehow lost sight of this in understanding human development.

Some of the best work in child development can be found in studies linking the context of a particular historical moment and a specific cultural community to general developmental processes and individual differences in response to that time and place (Elder and Conger, 2000; LeVine and others, 1994). The cultural content of what children do and think should be a part of our theoretical models and empirical methods, along with the more familiar abstracted and generalized psychological scales and assessments. Children do specific, particular, concrete cultural activities. Those activities have a script, norms, and cultural goals organizing them. Children do specific kinds of work and fulfill obligations that are embedded in particular relationships and systems of moral beliefs that make them feel that they are obliged to do them. Those who think about development in this way—as a fully contextualized, comparative social science—will enjoy reading the chapters in this volume. Those who are curious and interested more in the topics of the chapters—family assistance and the sense of obligation—will discover new, useful, and productive ways to think about development in context.

These chapters focus on a topic surprisingly underappreciated in developmental psychology: family responsibility, obligation, and the flows of moral and material capital between the generations from child to parents as well as parents to children. They also focus on adaptive problems and cultural goals that really matter to families and to our society for survival and well-being, such as children's everyday competence to manage a family and household economy and doing well in school. Each chapter illuminates the important roles of family responsibility, obligation, and the flows of moral and material capital between the generations.

Most developmental research emphasizes investment in children— stimulating them in home, school, and community for future productive success, for example—rather than on children investing in their families and communities. Yet we know that competence in assisting others can provide a sense of maturity and pride in children, that making a civic contribution can teach political as well as personal lessons, and that this experience is vital for working families who need children who can and will help. It is a matter of family survival and sustaining a family routine that children learn and can be relied on in this way.

This is of no surprise if we consider the findings from cross-cultural studies of children's development. Parental and child work and workload are important predictors of developmental transitions, social behavior, and cognitive development. The shift that occurs between ages five and seven, for example, is not only a change in cognitive and self-understanding; it is a cultural and familial transition as well, marked around the world by increasing expectations that children will not only assist but manage important parts of family life: caretaking of younger children, cooking, home safety, teaching, and other crucial tasks (Sameroff and Haith, 1996). A similar shift occurs in early adolescence; youth move toward peers and nonfamilial institutions, but also embody a family's hopes, social and material capital, and their future reproduction. In most cultures where children's contributions to family work has been examined ethnographically, working is a normal, expected part of a child's cultural pathway. A child who was not doing important tasks would be the marked category (What is the problem in that family? would be asked) rather than child work being unusual enough to be of concern as potentially problematic.

These chapters take children's work as a family contribution seriously. Workload can be considered from several points of view: sheer caloric expenditure and effort, time needed to do tasks, the calling up and organization of resources needed for domestic tasks, and the managerial and organizational complexity of the tasks children are asked to do. Some tasks entail doing other tasks (Burton, Brudner, and White, 1977)—that is, there is a functional efficiency to do them together. If you are already at home, it is more likely that you will do other tasks done in and around the home; if you are going to do the cooking, you are more likely to be responsible for buying the food, storing it, scheduling meals, and so forth. The subjective experience of doing tasks is also important. Is it felt as a burden, as unfair, as an important responsibility, or as part of the flow of everyday life that gives pleasure and satisfaction? Interesting data from children and parents about the experience of obligations and work can be found in these chapters.

Children acquire many of their work skills in the midst of family and community life as apprentices (Rogoff, 1990). They imitate, have the chance to practice work in context, and learn from other children through observation rather than through didactic instruction from adults in individualized, formal institutions like schools. Monitoring is usually done in context, while work is going on. The consequences of success and mistakes are concrete and immediate, matter to others who matter to the child, and build cumulatively in difficulty. Learning and doing family and neighborhood tasks in these ways is likely how children throughout cultural history acquired most of the competencies they needed for successful adaptation. The chapters in this volume capture some of these kinds of apprentice-like ways children become and feel competent in the contemporary world. Apprenticeship and obligation continue to be critical features of and for children's acquisition of valued and needed skills.

Crouter, Head, Bumpus, and McHale present a model of what encourages, in mothers' minds and in their practices, the use of boys and girls for domestic work in our culture. Their study suggests four processes or mechanisms that encourage mothers to rely on children to help and to lean more on daughters for home tasks: mothers' workloads are heavy; there is a cultural script for women and girls to do domestic work; mothers and daughters are close and daughters offer to help; and boys are not worth the trouble to try and bargain with in order to get them to do housework—this last an economic and bargaining hypothesis to help account for gender differences. Each of these mechanisms has cross-cultural support. Minturn and Lambert (1964), Whiting and Whiting (1975), and Whiting and Edwards (1988) found that heavier maternal workload and maternal responsibility for the domestic domain and for provisioning of children meant that children were given more responsibility for family economic tasks. Boys were too; however, boys more often had tasks to do outside the domestic sphere (herding, farmwork, trading, school). Boys in middle childhood were least likely to do domestic work, although they did do so if girls were not available. Workloads of fathers did not have a similar effect on children as long as the cultural script for domestic work did not require substituting domestic work for outside work and as long as fathers were not expected to manage the domestic domain. The tendency of children to imitate and practice what those similar (near in age, gender, interests, and other characteristics) to them do, rather than what those more different from them do, is likely also an important mechanism leading to the modeling of domestic tasks by girls of other girls and older women (Maccoby, 1998).

The low family size of Crouter's Pennsylvania sample compared to other countries means that there are fewer children available to help. Many communities around the world have culturally prepared ways to provide help for families and ensure that children have important work experiences. Child lending for periods of time, fostering children out to kin or wealthier families, time-limited adoptions of children into families needing a child's labor or assistance for some years, and full adoptions are widespread practices in many communities around the world. These shared responsibilities for caring for and managing children by a network of kin explicitly recognize the value of children's work, as well as the shared obligations for children's development (Serpell, 1993). At its best, such pathways enhance children's sense of community attachment and life chances, but children can also be exploited and denied opportunities in life.

Work obligations are shared among siblings in Crouter's sample. American cultural scripts for sibling relationships are not very clear and marked as important compared to scripts for gender roles, achievement, or parenting. Americans do not culturally elaborate sibling relationships nearly to the extent other cultures do. Sibling relationships are the idealized model for lifelong closeness in some communities, preferred to spousal or mother-child relationships (Marshall, 1983; Weisner, 1987). We certainly have extensive sibling caretaking in American society, but do not mark it or valorize it or research it nearly to the same extent as we do parental care, day care, and self-care.

The cross-cultural solution to the problems American mothers face in organizing domestic work is often to put an older girl in charge: if there are too many conflicts or the work is not being done, parents question, punish, or negotiate with the older children who are responsible. Little bargaining takes place directly between boys and their parents in such a system, for instance, although both siblings and parents certainly experience resentment, jealousy, and ambivalence. But if (as is true in the American middle-class cultural model of development and parenting) bargaining is set up as dyadic and nonhierarchical and if children are given cultural status as a coequal interlocutor with parents, then children have strong bargaining positions, as they seem to in many of the Pennsylvania families.

Fuligni shows the extent to which school achievement is related to factors in addition to classroom and teacher input and student abilities (although these surely do matter): the sense of family obligation and responsibility. Just as for domestic tasks, intergenerational family obligation is a very real practical matter around the world for family survival. Indeed, literacy and numeracy are the core subsistence tasks of the contemporary world, with the same concern and anxieties about them that other communities might have given to hunting, farming skills, pastoralism, trade, or ritual expertise. Absent reliable banks and credit, and often absent a reliable local or national police and security institution, kin remain the first, and often only, resource for families in much of the world. The psychological experience of shame and guilt when family obligations are not honored can be deep, painful, and consequential for people.

Family obligation may be diffused, less monitored, and weaker in the contemporary world, but it remains an important motivational force. Motivation is not only an internal individual state, but also a constructed experience within a cultural pathway. The experiences that children have of obligation and a need to persist in tasks they may not like, for example, are constituted both by a cultural schema and life pathway in a family and by the person engaged in that pathway. The schema of school success for many of the immigrant children in these studies is motivational in that it is a shared cultural-familial script, internalized in self and identity, and attached to strong feelings. In this way, cultural scripts, schemas, and pathways motivate action and can usefully be thought of as motives (D'Andrade, 1995).

In Fuligni's interviews, obligation leads to a willingness to stay with subjects like math that youth may not like, even when students in high school become disenchanted with education generally and see little practical value. The respect of youths for parents and extended kin translates into economic and personal sacrifice and influence. Clearly many of these youths do desire to support their families. Note that Fuligni's data show that actual academic achievement only weakly follows aspirations and expectations based on family obligation. But sheer persistence and reciprocated family support for further academic work help some of these students regardless. Assistance, respect, and support have different implications for academic persistence and achievement. Family monitoring and investment in sons and daughters imply control as well as a feeling of support.

Lassonde's study exemplifies how much the idea of family obligation with regard to schooling and the work lives of youth is historically and culturally entangled. The Italian immigrant story Lassonde tells for southern Italian immigrants in New Haven before and after World War I begins with an outline of the secular trends in the United States concerning cultural and historical expectations regarding success and schooling among Italian immigrants. He reviews historical changes in schooling (starting and completing high school only gradually becomes normative), gender (girls began taking clerical courses for their careers yet then were out in the community, unmonitored, with boys), and the economy (the depression devastated these immigrant families, and the needs for wage versus clerical work changed). The cultural schemas of family respect, obligation, and control also were changing (for example, marriage alters which family one is obligated to—but differently for boys and girls), and the control of wages and sexuality by families had different implications for each gender. Moral codes themselves were changing (the good and right path in life imagined by Italians at first opposed but then over the generations gradually incorporated what American society has to offer).

Lassonde provides a rich and contextualized example of the close connections between changes in the political economy in the United States (schooling beyond grade 8 is more and more expected as normative over time) and the way class and ethnicity change these expectations (unschooled immigrant parents are suspicious of formal schooling and are unprepared and unwelcome in it compared with schooled immigrants with a higher socioeconomic status). Utilitarian views of school were very important in the cultural models of these Italian families, just as they are among Fuligni's immigrant families. What counted as good-enough school achievement was a negotiated settlement between parents and children and the local community (a grade of C was fine if no college pathway was likely; when grades were too high, it led to problems with fulfilling other important family obligations). There were also variations among the immigrant families due to selective school and teacher investment and varying home literacy environments. Lassonde and Fuligni show how narrow are our judgments of school and family influences on school achievement outcomes and the potential abilities of youth if our understanding is based solely on school grades taken as the sum of teacher input plus student ability.

Although, as Lassonde says, age grading and school engagement emerged out of cultural and historical processes, rather than being "natural," the processes he and the other authors discover are found widely around the world. Although the obligations expected and assistance given by children and youth vary, the yoked developmental transitions linking youth and their parents actually are quite widespread around the world. Parents (and others where there is shared support and management by adults other than parents) are involved in arranging marriages (or preparing their children for their own mate choice by investing in children and making sure children invest in their family), regulating job choices of youth, and selectively making judgments about their children's aptitudes. Parents' lives are going through a change along with the changes in their teenagers' lives: parents are entering some version of midlife, or the beginning of the reproductive and intergenerational transitions in the continuity of the family (Shweder, 1998). Of course, midlife, like adolescence, varies around the world and throughout history as a life stage, and it may not even be a culturally recognized, marked category. Yet almost everywhere, there is a yoked transition linking parents and youth as youth leave or prepare to leave the household and as parents begin or reach the end of their parenting years. The parental goal of ensuring intergenerational success and the moral and material continuity of one's family surely is a very wide, if not universal, concern. This shared human concern underlies the diverse ways youth fulfill obligations and give assistance to their family and society, as well as shaping the psychological experiences of parents and their children engaging in this project.

References

Burton, M. L., Brudner, L. A., and White, D. R. "A Model of the Sexual Division of Labor." *American Ethnologist,* 1977, *4,* 227–251.

D'Andrade, R. *The Development of Cognitive Anthropology.* Cambridge, England: Cambridge University Press, 1995.

Elder, G. H., Jr., and Conger, R. D. *Children of the Land: Adversity and Success in Rural America.* Chicago: University of Chicago Press, 2000.

Kessen, W. "Rubble or Revolution: A Commentary." In R. H. Wozniak and K. W. Fischer (eds.), *Development in Context: Acting and Thinking in Specific Environments.* Hillsdale, N.J.: Erlbaum, 1993.

LeVine, R. A., and others. *Child Care and Culture: Lessons from Africa.* Cambridge, England: Cambridge University Press, 1994.

Maccoby, E. E. *The Two Sexes: Growing Up Apart, Coming Together.* Cambridge, Mass.: Harvard University Press, 1998.

Marshall, M. (ed.). *Siblingship in Oceania: Studies in the Meaning of Kin Relations.* Lanham, Md.: University Press of America, 1983.

Minturn, L., and Lambert, W. W. *Mothers of Six Cultures: Antecedents of Child Rearing.* New York: Wiley, 1964.

Rogoff, B. *Apprenticeship in Thinking: Cognitive Development in Social Context.* New York: Oxford University Press, 1990.

Sameroff, A., and Haith, M. (eds.). *The Five to Seven Year Shift: The Age of Reason and Responsibility.* Chicago: University of Chicago Press, 1996.

Serpell, R. *The Significance of Schooling: Life-Journeys in an African Society.* Cambridge, England: Cambridge University Press, 1993.

Shweder, R. (ed.). *Welcome to Middle Age! (and Other Cultural Fictions).* Chicago: University of Chicago Press, 1998.

Weisner, T. S. "Socialization for Parenthood in Sibling Caretaking Societies." In J. Lancaster, A. Rossi, J. Altmann, and L. Sherrod (eds.), *Parenting Across the Life Span.* Hawthorne, N.Y.: Aldine de Gruyter, 1987.

Whiting, B. B., and Edwards, C. P. *Children of Different Worlds: The Formation of Social Behavior.* Cambridge, Mass.: Harvard University Press, 1988.

Whiting, B. B., and Whiting, J.W.M. *Children of Six Cultures: A Psycho-Cultural Analysis.* Cambridge, Mass.: Harvard University Press, 1975.

THOMAS S. WEISNER is professor of anthropology in the Departments of Psychiatry (Center for Culture and Health) and Anthropology, University of California at Los Angeles.

Index

Abruzzi, Italy, 45

Adolescents: academic motivation of, 62–63, 64–70; changes in status of, 18; and effect of paid work, 18–19; reminders favored by, 16; study of, 63–70; value of English to, 68; value of math to, 68. *See also* Children

Adolescents, Asian: academic motivation of, 62–63, 64–70; attitudes toward family obligations, 64, 72–74; attitudes toward schooling, 62, 64, 72–74; versus European American adolescents, 62–63, 67–70; motivation for schooling, 62–63; study of, 63–70; value of English to, 68; value of math to, 68

Adolescents, Latin American, 62–70; academic motivation of, 62–63, 64–70; attitudes toward family obligations, 64, 72–74; attitudes toward schooling, 62, 64, 72–74; versus European American adolescents, 62–63, 67–70; motivation for schooling, 62–63; value of English to, 68; value of math to, 68

Age grading, 43, 82

Age of family member: and changes in contributions, 20; and contributions, 11; and effect of mothers' employment on contributions, 31–32, 33–34, 36–37; Italian immigrants' attitudes about, 47–49

Alexander, J. T., 57

Altenbaugh, R. J., 45, 55

Antill, J., 10, 29

Approach-avoidance motivation, 72

Apulia, Italy, 45

Artisans, children of, 49

Asian culture, 61–62

Asians. *See* Adolescents, Asian

Attendance, school, 46, 48

Attitudes: of Asian American adolescents toward schooling, 62, 64–67; of children, 32, 33–36, 37–38; of ethnic groups toward schooling, 44; of females, 33–34, 37–38; of Italian females toward schooling, 57; of Italian immigrants about age, 47–49; of Italian immigrants toward schooling, 45–46, 47, 48, 55, 56–57; of Italian males toward schooling, 56–57; of Latin American adoles-

cents toward schooling, 62, 64–67; of males, 33–34, 37–38; measurement of, 29

Austin, E. W., 51

Australia, 6–7, 7, 16

Avoidance motivation, 72

Bakke, E. W., 56

Banfield, E. C., 46

Bankston, C. L., 62

Bartko, T., 18, 29

Barton, J. J., 44

Basilicata, Italy, 45

Becker, G. S., 55, 56

Beijing, 16

Bell, R. M., 50

Berk, S. F., 6

Betteti, M., 54

Birth order, 51. *See also* Firstborn children; Second-born children

Blame, 15

Bock, D., 73

Bodnar, J., 51

Bowen, W. G., 73

Bowes, J. A., 10, 11, 14, 16

Brinkerhoff, D. B., 7, 24, 25

Brudner, L. A., 79

Buckley, S., 24, 26

Bumpus, M. F., 2, 23, 29, 79

Burton, M. L., 79

Calabria, Italy, 45

Campania, Italy, 45

Canada, 7

Caplan, N., 62

Cashmore, J., 7

Chen, M. J., 16, 17

Child, I. L., 53, 54, 56–57, 58

Children: age grading among, 43; age of, 11; attitudes of, 32, 33–36, 37–38; in Australia, 7; in Canada, 7; development of responsibility in, 7, 77–79, 80; and exceptions to rules, 12; firstborn, 28, 29, 39; household competence of, 7; and principles of mothers, 12–13; in rural families, 7; second-born, 28, 29, 39; in urban families, 7. *See also* Adolescents

Children, Italian: of artisans, 49; and attitudes toward schooling, 56–57; contributions of, 49, 50–51; and effect of birth order on schooling, 51; and effect of gender on schooling, 51–55; paid work of, 53; play of, 48–49; population in New Haven, Connecticut, 46–47, 55, 57–58; school performance of, 44–45; types of schooling for, 49

Children's Attitudes Toward Women Scale, 29

Chilman, C. S., 61

China, 16–17

Chores. *See* Contributions

Choy, M. H., 62

Chrisman, K., 12

Chudacoff, H. P., 43

Circumstances of contributions, 8–9, 14

Clark, M. S., 12

Clubb, J. M., 51

Cohen, L., 7

Cole, M., 43

Cole, S. R., 43

Coltrane, S., 26

Competence, household, 7, 18

Compulsory attendance, 46, 48

Confucianism, 61

Conger, R. D., 77

Connecticut, 44–45, 45–47

Connecticut State Employment Service, 57

Consensus, 8

Contadini. See Italian immigrants

Contributions: and child development, 77, 79; circumstances of, 8, 9, 14; and culture, 78, 80–81; definition of, 5, 6; description of, 8; development of framework for, 8–9; distinctions among, 11–12, 13–14; division of, 32–36, 37, 38; and effect of age, 20; and effect of gender, 23–24, 27, 32–36, 37, 38, 80; emotional help as, 11; and expectations of parents, 7; family work as, 11; of fathers, 25; feelings about, 9; of females, 7, 10; and gender, 7, 10; of males, 7, 10; and mothers' cleaning up after others, 12–13; movability versus person specificity, 10–17; need for framework for, 5; person specificity of, 8, 9, 10–17; perspectives on, 6–7; and principles of mothers, 12–13; and role overload, 29; in rural families, 7; self-care tasks as, 11; of siblings, 14, 25–27,

30–36, 37, 38, 39; study of daughters', 25–32; style of, 8, 9; in urban families, 7; as vehicle for negotiation, 17; and work hours, 29; and work pressure, 29. See also Work, paid

Contributions, adolescent: in Australia, 16; and blame, 15; checking for completion of, 15; in Czechoslovakia, 16; gender differences in, 15; in Hungary, 16; lack of research on, 1; in Sweden, 16

Cotton, S., 7, 10, 29

Couples, 14

Covello, L., 46, 47, 48–49, 50, 51, 52, 53–55

Crouter, A. C., 2, 18, 23, 24, 25, 26, 29, 33, 34, 79

Culture: of Asia, 61–62; and child development, 77–78, 80; of Latin America, 61–62; and motivation, 81; and schooling, 81–82; and siblings, 80

Cutts, N. E., 45

Czechoslovakia, 16

D'Andrade, R., 81

Dawes, L. J., 14

Deci, E. L., 71

Delaney, S., 10–11, 12

DeVault, I. A., 55

DeVault, M., 26, 37

Discipline, 50

Dual-earner families, 27

Eccles, J. S., 65, 73

Edwards, C. P., 79

Elder, G. H., Jr., 77

Elliot, A., 72

Emotional help, 11

English courses, 68

Ethnic groups, 44. *See also specific ethnic groups*

Exceptions to rules, 11–12

Expectations, parent, 7, 19

Fairness, 12

Families: and concepts of negotiation, 19; consensus in, 8; with dual incomes, 27; and feelings about contributions, 9; hierarchical patterns of, 19; requests in, 14; in rural areas, 7; settings of, 12; study of, 25–32; in urban areas, 7. See also Italian immigrants

Family obligations: of Asian American adolescents, 62–63; Asian Americans' attitudes toward, 64, 72–74; of Latin American adolescents, 62–63; Latin Americans' attitudes toward, 64, 72–74; and motivation, 67–70, 71–74, 81; schooling as, 62; study of, 64–70

Family work, 11

Fass, P. S., 57

Fathers: contributions of, 25; in Penn State Family Relationships Project, 28; work demands on, 30, 79–80

Feldman, E. E., 57

Females: attitudes of, 33–34, 37–38; and checking on job completion, 15; contributions of, 7, 10; effect of mothers' employment on, 24–25, 36–37, 79; firstborn, 28, 29, 31, 39; in Penn State Family Relationships Project, 28; relationships with mothers, 26, 79; second-born, 28, 29, 31, 39; study of, 25–32; views of paid work by, 15–16

Females, Italian: and attitudes toward schooling, 57; contributions of, 49, 50–51; and effect of gender on schooling, 51–55; and marriage, 52, 53

Ferree, M. M., 26

Firstborn children, 28, 29, 31, 39. See also Birth order; Second-born children

Flanagan, C., 20

Framework for contributions, 5, 8–9

Fuligni, A. J., 1, 2, 3, 61–62, 63, 64, 68, 69, 80–81

Galantuomo class, 46

Gender: attitudes about, 32, 33–36, 37–38; and checking on job completion, 15; and differences in contributions, 7, 10, 15; effect on contributions, 23–24, 32–36, 37, 38, 80; and movability of contributions, 13–14; and views of paid work, 15–16

Giacomini, B., 52–53

Glenn, S. A., 51

Goncu, A., 6, 7

Goode, W. J., 26

Goodnow, J. J., 1, 5, 6, 7, 8, 9, 10, 11, 12, 14, 15, 16, 17, 23, 29

Grolnik, W. S., 71

Grusec, J. E., 7

Haith, M., 78

Head, M. R., 2, 23, 79

Helms-Erikson, H., 29, 33

Ho, D.Y.F., 61

Hogan, D. J., 44

Household competence, 7, 18

Hungary, 16

Huston, A. C., 38

Italian immigrants: and attitudes about age, 47–49; and attitudes toward schooling, 45–46, 47, 48, 55, 56–57; and discipline, 50; and effect of birth order on schooling, 51; and effect of gender on schooling, 51–55; family economy of, 45, 46, 54; illiteracy among, 45; and marriage, 52, 53; and paid work of children, 53; population in New Haven, Connecticut, 46–47, 55, 57–58; research on, 44; types of schooling for, 49; upward mobility of, 44. See also Families

Italy, 45–46

Ja, D. Y., 61

Karantzas, G., 10, 11

Kessel, F., 17

Kessen, W., 77

Kett, J. F., 43

Kirk, G. W., Jr., 51

Kitayama, S., 74

Knight, R., 7

Lam, M., 61–62, 64, 69

Lambert, W. W., 79

Larson, R. W., 23, 24

Lassonde, S., 2, 43, 44, 46, 55, 81

Latin American culture, 61–62

Latin Americans. See Adolescents, Latin American

Lave, J., 7

Lawrence, J. A., 1, 5, 10, 11

Lazerson, M., 44

Lebanese mothers, 7

Lessons of mothers, 12–13

Levine, D., 45, 77

Li, Q. S., 16

Li, Y., 16

Lin, S-H., 10, 11

Maccoby, E. E., 80

Maguire, M. C., 29

Males: attitudes of, 33–34, 37–38; and checking on job completion, 15;

contributions of, 7, 10; effect of mothers' employment on, 26–27, 79; first-born, 28, 29, 31, 39; negotiation by, 80; in Penn State Family Relationships Project, 28; second-born, 28, 29, 31, 39; views of paid work by, 15–16

Males, Italian: and attitudes toward schooling, 56–57; contributions of, 49, 50–51; and effect of gender on schooling, 51–55

Manke, B., 24, 25, 26

Markus, H. R., 74

Marriage, 52, 53

Marshall, M., 80

Martin, C. M., 38

Math courses, 68

McHale, S., 2, 18, 23, 24, 25, 26, 29, 33, 34, 79

Mead, M., 48

Medrich, E. A., 24, 26

Menaghan, E. G., 25

Miller, P. J., 17

Minturn, L., 79

Mirel, J. E., 43

Mistry, J., 6, 7

Modell, J., 51, 57

Models of motivation, 70–71, 72

Montemayor, R., 8

Montgomery, D., 55

Moos, R. H., 29

Mosier, C., 6, 7

Mothers: in Australia, 6–7; in China, 16–17; and cleaning up after others, 12–13; effect of, employment on daughters, 24–25, 36–37, 79; and exceptions to rules, 11–12; lessons of, 12–13; in Penn State Family Relationships Project, 28; principles of, 12–13; relationships with daughters, 26, 79; and self-care tasks, 11; study of, 25–32; work demands on, 30

Motivation: approach-avoidance, 72; avoidance, 72; and culture, 81; and family obligations, 67–70, 71–74, 81; models of, 70–71, 72; obligation-related, 71, 72; and respect, 72, 73; for schooling in Asian American adolescents, 62–63, 64–70; for schooling in Latin American adolescents, 62–63, 64–70; study of, 64–70

Movability: and distinctions among tasks, 11–12; versus person specificity, 10–17;

and requests, 14; and room for change, 19; and siblings, 14

Myers, J. K., 46–47

National Institute of Child Health and Human Development, 3

Negotiation: in China, 17; contributions as vehicle for, 17; familial concepts of, 19; and family hierarchical patterns, 19; by males, 80; and schooling, 82

New Haven, Connecticut, 44–45, 45–47

New Haven Board of Education, 45, 46, 55, 58

Noland, W. E., 56

Nordli, W., 57

Obligation-related motivation, 71, 72

Olneck, M. R., 44

Orsi, R. A., 50

Palmieri, J., 52

Parcel, T. B., 25

Parents: and checking on completion of contribution, 15; elderly, 11; expectations of, 7; responsibility for, 11. *See also* Fathers; Mothers

Pay rates, 1939–1960, 55–56

Penn State Family Relationships Project, 27–29

Perlmann, J., 44, 45

Perry-Jenkins, M., 18, 25

Person specificity, 8, 9, 10–17

Play of Italian children, 48–49

Population of Italian immigrants in New Haven, Connecticut, 46–47

Racca, V., 46–47, 50, 52–53

Rawls, H. A., 15

Reilly, M. D., 29

Reminders, 16

Repetti, R. L., 25

Requests, 14

Research: on effects of mothers' employment on contributions, 25; on Italian immigrants, 44; lack of focus on adolescent contributions, 1; Penn State Family Relationships Project, 27–29

Respect, 72, 73

Responsibility: development of, 7; for elderly parents, 11; for emotional help, 11; as lesson of mothers, 12–13

Rheingold, H. L., 6

Rogoff, B., 6, 7, 79
Roizen, J., 24, 26
Role overload, 29
Role Overload Scale, 29
Rubin, V., 24, 26
Ruble, D. N., 38
Rules, 11–12
Rural families, 7
Rury, J. L., 55
Russell, G., 10, 29
Ryan, J., 10, 11
Ryan, R. M., 71

Sameroff, A., 78
San Francisco, 63
Schooling: Asian American adolescents'
    attitudes toward, 62, 64–67; attitudes
    toward, 44; and compulsory attendance,
    46, 48; and culture, 81–82; and effect of
    birth order in Italian families, 51; and
    effect of gender in Italian families,
    51–55; ethnic groups' attitudes toward,
    44; Italian females' attitudes toward, 57;
    Italian immigrants' attitudes toward,
    45–46, 47, 48, 55, 56–57; Italian males'
    attitudes toward, 56–57; Italian versus
    American, 50; in Italy, 45–46; Latin
    American adolescents' attitudes toward,
    62, 64–67; motivation for, 62–63,
    64–70; and negotiation among family
    members, 82; and pay rates, 1939–1960,
    55–56; performance of Italian children
    in, 44–45; types of, in Italian family, 49
Second-born children, 28, 29, 31, 39. See
    also Birth order
Seery, B. L., 25, 26
Self-care tasks, 11
Self-determination theory, 71
Serpell, R., 80
Shon, S. P., 61
Shure, M. B., 11
Shweder, R., 82
Siblings: age of, 31–32, 33–34, 36–37;
    and culture, 80; and division of labor,
    32–36, 37, 38; firstborn, 28, 29, 31,
    39; and movability of contributions,
    14; in Penn State Family Relationships
    Project, 28; second-born, 28, 29, 31,
    39; study of, 25–27, 30–36, 37, 38–39
Smetana, J., 18, 19
Smith, J. E., 53

Smith, T. L., 44
Starrels, M. E., 26
Status, adolescent, 18
Staub, E., 6
Straus, J. A., 6, 18–19
Style, 8, 9
Suárez-Orozco, C., 62
Suárez-Orozco, M. M., 62
Sweden, 16

Taylor, A. J., 14, 16
Theory, self-determination, 71
Thernstrom, S., 44
Tseng, V., 61–62, 63, 64, 69
Tucker, C. J., 25, 34

Uba, L., 1994
Updegraff, K. A., 33
Urban families, 7

Vecoli, R. J., 50
Verma, S., 23, 24

Warton, P. M., 9, 11, 12, 14, 15, 16
Weisner, T., 3, 77, 80
Wenger, E., 7
West, C., 26
White, D. R., 79
White, L. K., 7, 24, 25
Whitelaw, J. B., 47
Whiting, B., 23, 79
Whiting, J., 23, 79
Whitmore, J. K., 62
Wigfield, A., 73
William T. Grant Foundation, 3
Williams, P. H., 50, 51, 53
Work, paid: and effect on adolescents,
    18–19; of Italian children, 53; views
    of, 15–16. See also Contributions
Work demands: aspects of, 29; on fathers,
    30, 79–80; on mothers, 30
Work Environment Scale, 29
Work hours, 29
Work pressure, 29

Yans-McLaughlin, V., 52

Zelizer, V., 6
Zhou, M., 62
Zimmerman, D., 26

SINGLE ISSUE SALE

For a limited time save 10% on single issues! Save an additional 10% when you purchase three or more single issues. Each issue is normally $28.00.

Please see the next page for a complete listing of available back issues.

Mail or fax this completed form to: Jossey-Bass, A Wiley Company
989 Market Street • Fifth Floor • San Francisco CA 94103-1741

CALL OR FAX

Phone 888-378-2537 or 415-433-1740 *or Fax* 800-605-2665 or 415-433-4611 (*attn customer service*)
BE SURE TO USE PRIORITY CODE DF2 TO GUARANTEE YOUR DISCOUNT!

Please send me the following issues at $25.20 each.

Important: please include series initials and issue number, such as CD88

1. CD _____

_____

_____

$ _____ TOTAL for single issues ($25.20 each)

_____ LESS 10% if ordering 3 or more issues

_____ SHIPPING CHARGES: SURFACE   Domestic Canadian
First Item $5.00 $6.50
Each Add'l Item $3.00 $3.00
For next-day and second-day delivery rates, call the number listed above.

$ _____ TOTAL (Add appropriate sales tax for your state. Canadian residents add GST)

Payment enclosed (U.S. check or money order only)

VISA, MC, AmEx Discover Card # _____ Exp. date _____

Signature _____

Day phone _____

Bill me (U.S. institutional orders only. Purchase order required)

Purchase order # _____

    Federal Tax ID. 135593032   GST 89102 8052

Name _____

Address _____

_____

_____

Phone _____ E-mail _____

For more information about Jossey-Bass, visit our website at: www.josseybass.com

OFFER EXPIRES MARCH 31, 2002.   **PRIORITY CODE = DF2**

OTHER TITLES AVAILABLE IN THE
NEW DIRECTIONS FOR CHILD AND ADOLESCENT DEVELOPMENT SERIES
William Damon, Editor-in-Chief

CD93   Supportive Frameworks for Youth Engagement, *Mimi Michaelson, Anne Gregor, Jeanne Nakamura*

CD92   The Role of Family Literacy Environments in Promoting Young Children's Emerging Literacy Skills, *Pia Rebello Britto, Jeanne Brooks-Gunn*

CD91   The Role of Friendship in Psychological Adjustment, *Douglas W. Nangle, Cynthia A. Erdley*

CD90   Symbolic and Social Constraints on the Development of Children's Artistic Style, *Chris J. Boyatzis, Malcolm W. Watson*

CD89   Rights and Wrongs: How Children and Young Adults Evaluate the World, *Marta Laupa*

CD88   Recent Advances in the Measurement of Acceptance and Rejection in the Peer System, *Antonius H. N. Cillessen, William M. Bukowski*

CD87   Variability in the Social Construction of the Child, *Sara Harkness, Catherine Raeff, Charles M. Super*

CD86   Conflict as a Context for Understanding Maternal Beliefs About Child Rearing and Children's Misbehavior, *Paul D. Hastings, Caroline C. Piotrowski*

CD85   Homeless and Working Youth Around the World: Exploring Developmental Issues, *Marcela Raffaelli, Reed W. Larson*

CD84   The Role of Peer Groups in Adolescent Social Identity: Exploring the Importance of Stability and Change, *Jeffrey A. McLellan, Mary Jo V. Pugh*

CD83   Development and Cultural Change: Reciprocal Processes, *Elliot Turiel*

CD82   Temporal Rhythms in Adolescence: Clocks, Calendars, and the Coordination of Daily Life, *Ann C. Crouter, Reed W. Larson*

CD81   Socioemotional Development Across Cultures, *Dinesh Sharma, Kurt W. Fischer*

CD80   Sociometry Then and Now: Building on Six Decades of Measuring Children's Experiences with the Peer Group, *William M. Bukowski, Antonius H. Cillessen*

CD79   The Nature and Functions of Gesture in Children's Communication, *Jana M. Iverson, Susan Goldin-Meadow*

CD78   Romantic Relationships in Adolescence: Developmental Perspectives, *Shmuel Shulman, W. Andrew Collins*

CD77   The Communication of Emotion: Current Research from Diverse Perspectives, *Karen Caplovitz Barrett*

CD76   Culture as a Context for Moral Development, *Herbert D. Saltzstein*

CD75   The Emergence of Core Domains of Thought: Children's Reasoning About Physical, Psychological, and Biological Phenomena, *Henry M. Wellman, Kayoko Inagaki*

CD74   Understanding How Family-Level Dynamics Affect Children's Development: Studies of Two-Parent Families, *James P. McHale, Philip A. Cowan*

CD73   Children's Autonomy, Social Competence, and Interactions with Adults and Other Children: Exploring Connections and Consequences, *Melanie Killen*

CD72   Creativity from Childhood Through Adulthood: The Developmental Issues, *Mark A. Runco*

CD69   Exploring Young Children's Concepts of Self and Other Through Conversation, *Linda L. Sperry, Patricia A. Smiley*

CD67   Cultural Practices as Contexts for Development, *Jacqueline J. Goodnow, Peggy J. Miller, Frank Kessel*

CD65   Childhood Gender Segregation: Causes and Consequences, *Campbell Leaper*

CD46   Economic Stress: Effects on Family Life and Child Development, *Vonnie C. McLoyd, Constance Flanagan*

CD40   Parental Behavior in Diverse Societies, *Robert A. LeVine, Patrice M. Miller, Mary Maxwell West*